D0675256

The Horrors We Bless

FACETS

Selected Titles in the Facets Series

The Horrors
We Bless

Rethinking the
Just-War Legacy

Daniel C. Maguire

Fortress Press
Minneapolis

THE HORRORS WE BLESS
Rethinking the Just-War Legacy

Biblical quotations from *The New English Bible with the Apocrypha: Oxford Study Edition* (London: Oxford University Press, 1970) are by permission of the publisher.

Cover design: Abby Hartman
Cover image: copyright © Benjamin Lowy/CORBIS.
    Used by permission.
Interior design: Timothy W. Larson
This book was set in Rotis Serif and Rotis Sans Serif.

Library of Congress Cataloging-in-Publication Data
Maguire, Daniel C.
    The horrors we bless : rethinking the just-war legacy / Daniel C. Maguire.
        p. cm.
    Includes bibliographical references.
    ISBN-13: 978-0-8006-3897-9 (alk. paper)
    ISBN-10: 0-8006-3897-2 (alk. paper)
    1. Just war doctrine. 2. War—Religious aspects—Christianity. I. Title.
BT736.2.M34 2007
241'.6242—dc22   2006038936

Manufactured in the U.S.A.
11   10   09   08   07   2   3   4   5   6   7   8   9   10

Contents

Preface

War is a form of state-sponsored violence. To challenge the seductive power of war that so grips and hobbles our imaginations, I open with five keynoters, tone-setters, and eye-openers: William Sloane Coffin, Albrecht Haushofer, Pope John Paul II, Peter Ustinov, and a ten-year-old Afghan boy named Muhammad Noor.

War is the coward's escape from the problems of peace.

— William Sloane Coffin Jr.

Albrecht Haushofer was imprisoned and executed by the Nazis for joining plots against Hitler. While in prison he reflected on how the Nazi court had found him "guilty." In his poem "Schuld" ("Guilt"), written while in shackles in prison, he admitted to a different kind of guilt, the guilt of not protesting early enough and loudly and clearly enough against the evils of his government. "I should have known my duty earlier, and called evil by its name more sharply—my judgment I kept flexible far too long." This man, who as J. Glenn Gray said, "had already atoned more than is required of most of us," went to his death convinced that his protest had been "nicht hart genug und klar" (not strong and clear enough)![1] His "guilt" indicts us all, numbed and complacent as we are while our governments wreak havoc in our name.

[We can] enrich our common heritage with a very simple discovery that is within our reach, namely that war is the most barbarous and least effective way of resolving conflicts.

— Pope John Paul II

Terrorism is the war of the poor and war is the terrorism of the rich.

— Peter Ustinov

A ten-year-old Afghan boy, Mohammed Noor, was having his Sunday dinner when an American bomb struck. He lost both eyes and both hands. Who, with this child in mind, would dare sing "God Bless America" to this child, the hymn that would make God a coconspirator with American war-makers? Who would wave an American flag in front of him? The sightless eyes of this child should haunt us to the end of our days and sear on our souls the absolute need not just to pray for peace, but to do something to make it happen. Even as I write, the United States is blinding and maiming innocent people and innocent soldiers coerced into battle by elites who sit back in safety. Silence and passivity in the face of this is unholy. The passivity of citizens is the life-blood of tyrants.

1
What Is War?

Is war inevitable, so woven into the fabric of our being that it always was and always will be? Some scholars think so, noting that humans have been at peace for only 8 percent of the past 3,400 years of recorded history.[1] Another study concludes pessimistically that wars are largely random catastrophes whose specific time and location we cannot predict but whose recurrence we must expect just as we expect earthquakes and hurricanes. This fatalism leads a writer in *American Scientist* to see the nations of the world as banging "against one another with no more plan or principle than molecules in an overheated gas."[2] George Santayana said that only death will free us from wars; and the Gospel of Matthew warns of "wars and rumors of wars," noting glumly that "such things are bound to happen" (Matt. 24:6).

Nonetheless, early Christians, during the first three hundred years of Christianity, were fairly unanimous in opposing this dismal view. They didn't see war as normal but as an outrage and even a sacrilege. Later they succumbed to the supposed "normalcy of war" and borrowed and baptized a set of principles and rules for war that came to be known as "the just-war theory." War, as this theory has been loosely used, is "just" if certain conditions and rules are observed. This can contribute to the view that war must be accepted as normal and a fact of life to be regulated as best we can. Yet, taken seriously, as we will see, the "just-war theory" is a deterrent to the rush to war and can serve the same goal sought by pacifists, the ending of war.

The hard and even daunting question is this: If war is the unleashing of violence against people and this generous but vulnerable earth, can you really make rules for that? Can you make rules for slaughter and mayhem? Is it not like trying to make rules for an orgy? Are not wars, like orgies, impatient of regulation? In fact, orgies may be more open to rules since they are supposedly based on free libidinal expression. (This would exclude rape, of course, which is an act of violence and power, not of uncontrolled lust.) History shows, however, that in the heat of what strategists call "military necessity," "the rules of war" tend to melt away.

War is state-sponsored violence. Can it ever be justified? Some people say no and are called *pacifists.* Others in the "just-war" tradition say that "it depends." Neither position *as usually presented* meets the tests of reality. There is a third way of viewing state-sponsored violence that gives us the best way of taming the demons of war and even bringing war to an end.

Sometimes police have to act violently, but they do so in a community context with legal and enforceable restrictions. *My thesis here is that state-sponsored violence can only be justified in a community context with legal and internationally enforceable restrictions comparable to the restraints we put upon our police.*

Is that hopelessly naïve?

Not at all.

In fact, after World War II, the nations of the world agreed on precisely that idea. The humane and much-needed idea that no war is "just" unless the violence is patterned on police work is brilliantly enshrined in the Charter of the United Nations.[3] Articles 2 and 51 of that Charter were meant to put an end to the traditional vigilante approach to war illustrated by Adolf Hitler as well as by the "preemptive-war" policy of George W. Bush. In the civilizing view of the United Nations, state-sponsored violence could only be just in a communitarian setting under the restraints of enforceable international law. The main reason that the United Nations was founded was to make this possible. The stirring preamble to the Charter begins: "We the peoples of the United Nations determined to save succeeding generations from the scourge of war, which twice in our lifetime has brought untold sorrow to human-kind . . . [are determined] to practice tolerance and live together in peace with one another as good neighbors, and to unite our strength to maintain international peace and security."

Many nations, such as the United States, have preferred vigilante warring and have frustrated the United Nations and its Charter. This is a sad irony since U.S. scholars and diplomats were among the principal shapers of this policing paradigm for justifying war.

International studies professor Richard Falk writes: "World War II ended with the historic understanding that recourse to war between states could no longer be treated as a matter of national discretion, but must be regulated to the extent possible through rules administered by international institutions. The basic legal framework was embodied in the U.N. Charter, a multilateral treaty largely crafted by American diplomats and legal advisers. Its essential feature was to entrust the Security Council with administering a prohibition of recourse to international force (Article 2, Section 4) by states except in circumstances of self-defense, which itself was restricted to responses to a prior 'armed attack' (Article 51), and only then until the Security Council had the chance to review the claim."[4]

Collective, multinational action, coordinated by the U.N., could also address internal problems of nations when crimes against humanity are ongoing, as in Darfur and Zimbabwe at this writing. Articles 43 and 45 of the U.N. Charter provide for this, though there has been little political will to do so. This use of the U.N., when in place and organized, would also act as a deterrent and would buttress resolutions of the Security Council just as the presence of a well-organized police force deters crime within a nation.[5] It has been successfully used, though the international will to do this, and to pay for it, has been weak. The creation of the U.N. was a heroic effort of the human race at a time when recurrent twentieth-century blood baths chastened our minds, if but for a moment.

Because of neglect of the ideas that motivated the founding of the U.N., the demonic power of war-as-policy continues its successful seduction like a devil that defies exorcism. Volumes have been written to describe war, from Carl von Clausewitz's famous "a continuation of policy . . . by other means" to the view that war is not "a continuation of policy" but is, rather, the self-destructive collapse of policy, a collective act of despair, a failure of imagination. We accept it as we accepted slavery for centuries, as a "right and necessary social institution."[6] In this view, we haven't evolved enough morally to see war for the atrocity it is. In between these two views, a myriad of other views have sprouted.

A New Look at This Thing Called "War"

It is a sad trick of the mind that makes us all too often ignore the *obvious*, so we'll begin with the obvious and then move to further critique. What is most obvious is that *war is dumb*. Given all the glory we ascribe to war and warriors, that charge may seem undignified and unfair. Let the record speak.

People like to find settled, ritualized ways of doing things; and that's what we do when we engage in the business of socialized slaughter. Going back to the fourteenth century we find that the Europeans had pretty much ritualized the standard operating procedure for organized fighting. Soldiers showed up on a field, dressed in their proper colors (so you could tell friend from foe). Then they had at one another until one side prevailed or until both sides collapsed and those left standing went home to spin the event as best they could.

Then, in 1346, things changed—or, rather, one side changed the ritual. The French nobles arrived for battle at Crecy bedecked in their normal fashion. The British, however, had come upon the longbow and realized that they did not need fancy knights to use it. They trained peasant longbowmen and mowed the French down from a safe distance.

One would think that such an onslaught would focus the mind of some of the French military geniuses. But no. Ten years later at

Poitier, "as if in a state of collective psycholog-ical denial," as social critic Barbara Ehrenreich puts it, they once again rode to their death in a hail of arrows.[7] Worse yet, the point was still not made and in 1415 they did the same stupid thing at Agincourt. It was then that it began to dawn on the French that this five-hundred-year protocol of charging knights was no lon-ger operative, and it was then it seems that they turned to a girl—Joan of Arc—to guide the hapless men to more effective modes of fighting.

Clearly this was not an epic of intelligence. It was, to return to our word, *dumb*.

We Americans might smirkingly view these debacles as relics of time past, not something that would be at home in our sophisticated modernity. But wait! Let us move from Crecy, Poitiers, and Agincourt to Iraq in 2003 and what do we see?

We see American forces arriving dressed and equipped for World War II. But, alas, there was no Nazi army awaiting them, dressed in appro-priate uniforms and using similar weapons. But there we were, like the French at Crecy, care-fully uniformed and easily identifiable targets. The noise of our military equipment could be heard from half a mile away. We were full of confidence. "Bring 'em on!" said our president. And, indeed, they did come "on."

We had tried this old-time warfare in the jungles of Vietnam and finally had to scramble out in defeat. Still, our leaders, like the medieval nobles of France, would give it another try in the Middle East. What we missed is that the enemy now swims invisibly in the sea of the populace, surfacing at will, and deciding which of our cumbersome machines will next be blasted into smithereens. The Iraqi people who did not enjoy being invaded did enjoy an unmatchable trinity of strategic advantages: *invisibility*, *versatility*, and *patience*. War had changed but our dummy leaders had not. The slow attrition of guerilla warfare commenced.

Adding to the dumbness here is the fact that in the Revolutionary War, the Americans took lessons from the Indians and adopted guerilla tactics. As one New Englander wrote in 1677: "In our first war with the Indians, God pleased to show us the vanity of our military skill, in managing our arms, after the European mode. Now we are glad to learn the skulking way of war."[8] The "skulking way of war" is precisely what we faced in Iraq and "the vanity of our military skill" is again revealed. We had forgotten the lessons learned in early America. Once again, *dumb*.

Guerilla warfare is the only viable response to a superpower, but it introduces a new danger into the wild history of war. As long as guerillas (or insurgents) are motivated by something like occupation, they cannot be defeated except by genocide. Counter-insurgency or counter-guerilla warfare veers toward massacre (which is incipient genocide). Since the guerillas swim invisibly in the ocean of the people, that ocean becomes the enemy. Massacres and attacks on the people (My Lai in Vietnam, or Haditha and Falluja in Iraq) follow as surely as the night the day. The desperation of invaders and occupiers faced with guerilla insurgency also leads to the immoral torture of prisoners. Indiscriminate attacks by insurgents lead to indiscriminate reprisals. This form of war is, as ever, "hell."

War changes constantly, from charging knights in bright armor to longbowmen with their arrows, from uniformed soldiers in armored planes and vehicles to guerilla warfare—such changes show that the mode of war is an artificial construct of human imagination. We make up different ways of doing it. This should raise questions. Why not have a duel between the two leaders of the countries involved and agree to abide by the result? Is that any sillier than having armies of coerced citizens from the lower economic classes out slaughtering one another while gouging and wrecking the rest of nature?

War, it seems, demands dumbness. It requires that we find ways of ignoring reality. It requires myths or it won't work. We have to create an "image of the enemy," since if we saw the human beings these "enemies" are—people like us with all of our hopes and foibles—we could not easily kill them. There are many examples in battles that show just how artificial the myths of war are, how "the image of the enemy" is an artificial concoction of myths and fabrications.

Political theorist Michael Walzer tells of an incident in World War I. The Germans and the French had been shooting at one another. One side or the other realized that it was Christmas Day 1914 and so they put down their weapons and started singing carols. The other side joined them and they came together singing and sharing drinks "in the no-man's land between their lines."[9] When this had ended, they returned to killing one another.

Philosopher J. Glenn Gray tells a similar story from World War II. American soldiers were guarding German prisoners, with rifles on the ready. Four of the Germans, who were a trained quartet, began humming a tune. Within a few minutes, the tense atmosphere changed. "The rifles were put down, some of them within easy reach of the captives. Everybody clustered closer and began to hum the melodies." They started to share cigarettes and show snapshots of loved ones at home. The mythic "image of the enemy" was no match for a song. Then the commanding officer arrived, "speechless with fury and amazement." Back came the rifles and the myth was forced back in place.[10] Reality broke through for a moment. And the reality was that these soldiers on both sides were victims, citizens forced into military thralldom with a false consciousness wrapped around them like a noose. The noose had loosened for a lucid moment, and they saw "the enemy" as flesh and blood, human comrades, caught in temporary madness not of their making.

These two incidents of soldiers slipping out of the myth are not exceptional. Studies of soldiers on the front lines in World War II showed that most of the men on the front line never fired their guns.[11] Men on firing squads have resisted pulling the trigger. Others are reported weeping as they did shoot.[12] All the military training to make these soldiers into obedient automatons often fails to imprint. Desertion is a common problem for commanders. Napoleon learned he could not camp near a forest or his troops would escape.[13] Michael Walzer has collected many stories of soldiers in various wars who suddenly became aware of the humanity of the soldier in their rifle scope and simply could not pull the trigger. In one case, a soldier saw through his scope an enemy soldier lighting a cigarette—something he himself wanted to do at that moment—and he decided he could not kill this fellow smoker. "The image of the enemy" faded.

In another case, a soldier spotted a naked "enemy" soldier and found he could not shoot him. Similar reactions came when soldiers spotted their enemies drinking coffee, or carelessly stopping to enjoy the fresh smell of spring.[14] In these moments, as George Orwell said, the alleged enemy is, all of a sudden, "visibly a fellow-creature, similar to yourself, and you don't feel like shooting at him."[15]

It has often been said that truth is the first casualty of war. War requires the death of truth because truth has a way of dissolving the myths that fire the engines and stoke the energies needed to wage war. In other words, war requires that we dumb down so that we do not have to face what it is that we are doing.

Sometimes the dumbness of socialized slaughter (war) shows up in ways where tragedy and comedy meet. Germany's foremost news magazine *Der Spiegel* features a critical article about George W. Bush's "crusade against evil." They designed a satirical cover using figures from American popular culture. President Bush was given a muscular Rambo body with weapons and ammunition belts. Dick Cheney became "The Terminator" while Condoleeza Rice was dressed as Xena, the Warrior Princess. Colin Powell was Batman, and former Secretary of Defense Donald Rumsfeld was Conan the Barbarian, holding a sword that was dripping with blood.

Daniel Coats, the U.S. Ambassador to Germany, immediately went to *Der Spiegel's* editorial office not to protest but to report that "the President was flattered." Mr. Coats requested thirty-three poster-size copies of the cover to be conveyed back to the White House since all those depicted wanted copies.[16] This is a commentary not just on our leadership. The satiric cover that "flattered" our leaders was drawn right out of the popular violent icons of Americana.

The political leaders in this farce were twice elected by American voters. Dumbness is not restricted to those in charge. "We the people" are also infatuated by the allures of "quick-fix" violence. "Today as never before in their history Americans are enthralled with military power,"[17] according to Andrew Bacevich, a retired West Point-trained officer and Vietnam veteran, now an eloquent critic of "the new American militarism."

In waging recent wars American politicians have been able to count on a broad base of popular support. Resistance to war has been called the "third rail" of American politics and few politicians want to touch it. Popularity ratings of leaders often rise when those leaders march to war—or, more precisely, send others to march to war. And so, as a general rule, it is tragically true: we get the leaders we deserve.

The Disguises of War

General William Tecumseh Sherman was surely right when he said that "war is hell." That was not dumb. With remarkable success, however, the disguisers and baptizers of war have framed it in such nontoxic tones, have so successfully defanged and anointed *war* with respectability that we use it in all sorts of innocent and lovely contexts: "the war on poverty," "the war on cancer," "the war on illiteracy," and so forth. The word has shuffled off its negative meaning and reality. Other words in our vocabulary have retained their negative meaning, for example, *rape.* We would not talk about raping illiteracy or starting a national rape of poverty. But warring against those things is fine. The word *war* has become a naturalized citizen in the culture and can be used metaphorically without stigma.

War can even be a form of armchair spectator entertainment. It is acceptable for people to become "Civil War buffs," or "Revolutionary War buffs." If people were to announce themselves as "prostitution buffs" or "necrophilia buffs," their perverted absorption in such human disasters would raise eyebrows. Not so with war. We so love violence that we use it for entertainment in film and literature. Violence has wooed us and won our hearts. That is why we are not shocked and are even enthused when our governments use it recklessly.

At the time of the U.S. invasion of Mexico, a young man, writing anonymously in the Cambridge *Chronicle* predicted with too much hope: "Human butchery has had its day. . . . And the time is rapidly approaching when the professional soldier will be placed on the same level as a bandit, the Bedouin, and the thug."[18] That day is not yet.

War is so sown into the sinews of our cultural imagination that it crops up in the gentlest of contexts. Science journalist Walter Sullivan, in his prize-winning book *We Are Not Alone*, writes beautifully of the intelligence of dolphins. He alludes to the possibility that we may someday be able to communicate extensively with them and train them for complex tasks. This tantalizing prospect took him immediately to war. Dolphins could be used "by one government to scout out the submarines of another . . . to smuggle bombs into enemy harbors . . . serve on underwater demolition teams . . . [be taught to] sneak up on hostile submarines and shout something into the listening gear." He notes worries, however, that the dolphins might demur, that "they might prove to be pacifists."[19] Their nonhuman consciousness might be less amenable to violence!

Our haughty species should be slow to speak demeaningly of "descending to the level of animals." The human being, says Erich Fromm, "is the only mammal who is a large scale killer and sadist."[20] He cites evidence that if we had the same aggressiveness as chimpanzees in their natural habitat, our world would be a kinder place by far.

The cases where violence does any good are rare. A policeman shooting a crazed gunman who is about to kill children in a playground with a rifle is a case of justifiable violence. When there is no alternative, violence can be justified in a controlled legal setting (at the international level in accord with the United Nations Charter, at the domestic level in a police context) because it prevents greater violence. Even in these circumstances, however, violence normally is counterproductive and unnecessary.

It is primitive to prefer violence to negotiation and peacemaking, but that seems our preference. Otherwise why would we put the burden of proof on the conscientious objector and not on the warrior? Why, too, would we do everything to block soldiers from being conscientious objectors? Those who are most likely to go beyond the "hype" and see the reality of war face major social stigma and criminal charges if they dare proclaim the war immoral.

Our addiction to violence shows up poignantly in our budget. Wisely does the Gospel say our treasure (budget) shows where our heart is (Matt. 6:21). We spend around ten thousand dollars a second on military killpower in the United States, while states go bankrupt and schools close early for lack of funds. One example points to our folly and our passion for military power.

To see stupid and sinful waste, let us visit the U.S.S. *Kitty Hawk*, a nuclear-powered aircraft carrier. It is impressive: almost three football fields long and towering as high as a twenty-story building. On board it has six thousand crew and seventy state-of-the-art aircraft. And it is never lonely. As part of a "carrier battle group" it is accompanied by an Aegis cruiser outfitted to knock down incoming missiles, several frigates and destroyers, and one or more submarines and supply vessels. "The United States has thirteen of these carrier battle groups. No other country has even one."[21] That should be embarrassing. It is like having the greatest football team in the world and no opponents. It is, of course, the product of the *more-arms-equals-more-secure* illusion that undergirds American addiction to war.

The poignant words that Deuteronomy 31 put into the mouth of God cry out to us: "I have set before you life, and I have set before you death. And I have begged you to choose life for the sake of your children." The Song of Moses could have been addressed to us: "Perverse and crooked generation, whose faults have proved you no children of his. Is this how you repay the Lord, you brutish and stupid people?" (Deut. 32:5-6). We "brutish and stupid people" in the United States are spending thirty-one million dollars an hour, twenty-four hours a day on military power. Military analysts say we could "earmark for [military spending] as much as the next ten largest military powers combined and still reduce Pentagon outlays by tens of billions of dollars per year."[22] Even spending as much as the next ten biggest military spenders combined is paranoid, and we could do fine with even a fraction of that. But stop and think of what we could do with that money if we were to point it toward life and not toward death. Let me give some examples.

We could immediately double the salaries of all of the elementary and high school teachers in the United States, the perennial orphans of our national conscience. We could then take some of the rest of that money and buy some munitions from the military (they have bombs to spare) and use those munitions to blow up every inferior school building in the country. We could have contests. The little girl that writes the best essay gets to push that handle down and watch the building crumble. In its place we'll build something beautiful, efficient, and worthy of our children.

With a mere forty to fifty billion dollars a year—what it costs to wage war for several months in Iraq—we could finance all public college and university education, making it all free to qualified students. This would be like a G.I. Bill of Rights for *all* citizens— totally free. (For every dollar spent on the G.I. Bill after World War II, the government got a return of almost seven dollars!)[23] With college costs rising, and federal grants to states for education shrinking, millions of students are being blocked out of a college education. This is a senseless waste of minds while military contractors are awash in cash. In more civilized Western nations, college education is free! (This is part of the secret of Ireland's rise in economic strength.)

Health care could be free for those who cannot afford a copay, and no one would be denied a medicine they need. This actually would save us money since when we leave over forty million people without health insurance it ends up costing more as their conditions deteriorate and require expensive emergency-room care. Health care for everyone and their children is a basic human right, like the right to be literate, and we can afford to give it to everyone. Our preference, however, is for bombs.

We were supposedly made in the image and likeness of God, but what images are we following? Not the image of God, not the image of peace. We could take another few million dollars an hour from military uselessness and bring our trains into the twenty-first century. American trains cannot even stay on the track, which is where you want to be if you're a train. And when they're on a track they don't go anywhere quickly. You have to go to Europe or to Japan to see modern trains. Americans invented, in fact, the magnetic levitation train. We invented the technology, the Japanese perfected it, and they have tested it going at 320 miles an hour.

We could then, working with other nations through the U.N., take more of those wasted military dollars and end hunger and thirst on the earth. That would fight terrorism. People don't crash airplanes and send suicide bombers against a nation bent on ending illiteracy, hunger, and thirst. Jeremiah 23 might have been talking to the American Empire when he said: "Their course is evil and their might is not right." That language applies to any empire, and ours is an empire placing its trust in weaponry and not in the compassion and good sense that builds peace. We are too "brutish and stupid" (Deut. 32:5-6) to see that all that weaponry does not make us safe. Being a military "superpower" does not make us safe; being a moral superpower known for our compassion would make us safe. The modest nations of the world have nothing to fear from terrorism, as historian and social critic Howard Zinn often reminds us.

It's a simple idea. Jeremiah would say: "You foolish and senseless people, who have eyes and see nothing, ears and hear nothing" (Jer. 5:21).

Revealingly, we talk about the strength of our nation in terms of our military kill-power, rather than by such things as a healthy trade balance, more equitable income distribution, high voter turnout, the availability of health care for all men, women, and children in the country, excellence in public and private schools, accessible drug-treatment programs, and reliable pension plans so that people can grow old in peace. If we are weak in these areas—and we are—we are weak indeed, even if we have the military capacity to kill everybody on this planet.

Americans like to think of themselves as number one. As one commentator puts it: "At least as measured by our capacity to employ violence we are indeed Number One."[24] Where we are not number one is in the fine art of diplomacy and peacemaking. Hands grown rough with bludgeoning are poor candidates for doing needlepoint.

How Did We Get So Dumb about War?

Some blame for the facile acceptance and even sanctification of war must go to the venerable and misused "just-war theory." This theory, developed over centuries, was a noble effort to minimize the harm of war. The theory had some successes and can be used to limit and block wars, but it has tended to be honored in word more than deed. The mischief of the "just-war theory" was that by putting the word *war* alongside the word *just*, it baptized war, making it seem rational and moral and good as long as certain rules are observed. It helped to rationalize war.

Just-war talk helped us to hide the reality of human and ecological devastation that war always involves. The abused word *war* has lost its sting; it is no longer descriptive of the horror we are wreaking when we "go to war." If the "just-war theory" were called the "justifiable-slaughter theory" or "the justifiable-violence theory," it would at least be honest. Maybe the slaughter and the human and ecological devastation we are planning are justifiable, but at least we would be honest in admitting what it is we are justifying. It would be language without *legerdemain*. In moral matters, the rush to euphemisms is always a sign of bad faith.

Military strategists, and ethicists embedded with them, drape an even thicker tissue of lies and euphemisms around military violence. They like to call it "the use of force." That sugarcoats it handsomely. *Force*, after all, is nice. A forceful personality, a forceful argument—these can be quite admirable. But an atomic bomb hitting the population centers of Hiroshima or Nagasaki or the brutal leveling of Falluja in Iraq or of settlement camps in Palestine needs a more honest word than *force*. *Force*, like *war*, is a malicious euphemism. It averts our eyes from the horrors described by Archbishop Desmond Tutu: "Some two million children have died in dozens of wars during the past decade. . . . This is more than three times the number of battlefield deaths of American soldiers in all their wars since 1776. . . . Today, civilians account for more than 90 percent of war casualties."[25]

We need a fresh look at the "just-war the-ory," a principal tool for making war look normal. Its use is widespread, even when not referred to as such, though it is more often used as a cover for stupid military adventures brought on by the failure to do the work that makes peace. Transforming that theory so that it truly serves peace is our goal.

2

The Strengths
and Weaknesses
of Just-War Theory

The "just-war theory" is the most common tool for deciding when a war is just. Even those who do not know its roots in Greek, Roman, and religious writings tend to use its categories in justifying the resort to the collective violence that we call war. It is usually divided into *jus ad bellum* (the right to go to war) and *jus in bello* (how you should behave when you get there). There is much in the doctrine that is admirable. The problem, however, is that given the passions of war, these well-meant restraints are easily and regularly trashed.

Noble effort that it was, "just-war" theory's main sin was its contribution to normalizing war, making war seem morally manageable and almost routine. Even Augustine saw that if you went to war you should do so "in a mournful mood," but if there are supposed rules in place to regulate and, as it were, to tame this violent enterprise, there seems less need for mourning. The rules of "just-war" theory in practice regularly gave a moral patina and sheen to activities that any ethics should condemn. That said, the need is not to jettison these rules but to update them and insist on their morally binding necessity. When fleshed out with an eye to the psychology, history, and science of war today, they can still serve the peacemaking agenda. They can stand as an obstacle to the facile resort to violence. They can place a massive burden of proof on the heads of war-makers.

Two things can be said, for starters, about the just-war theory: (1) taken seriously (even without revisions), it would condemn as immoral all the recent wars of the United States, and (2) it labors under Jean-Paul Sartre's judgment that the greatest evil of which we are capable is to treat as abstract that which is concrete. Augustine was one of the theory's architects and it reeks of his flawed contact with reality, as when he wrote that "love does not exclude wars of mercy waged by the good."[1] "Wars of mercy waged by the good" is euphemism in full bloom and smacks more of the library than the blood-soaked battlefield. Just-war theories, *if not revised and updated*, can be critiqued for deficits in the *psychology of war*, the *history of war*, and the *science of war*. All three deficits in traditional presentations of the theory will show up in the analysis and revisions that follow.

The main merit of just-war theory is its recognition that war is a horror and any defense of it bears the burden of proof. So the theory sets up tests that must be met for a war to be "just." Nothing could be more serious because if the war is not justifiable, the killing it involves is murder and those waging and fighting the war are murderers. *Murder, by definition, is killing for no justifiable reason.*

Note, too, that for a war to be justified, *all* of these criteria and tests must be met. Failure to pass even one of these tests makes the war unjust and murderous.[2] A war that is not justifiable is mass murder.

As the American Catholic Bishops said, these tests "require extraordinarily strong reasons for overriding the presumption *in favor of peace and against war.*"[3] These tests are the business of citizens as well as of government officials since citizens are meant to be the conscience of the nation. "Democracy is a way of distributing responsibility just as monarchy is a way of refusing to distribute it."[4] Citizens who avoid responsibility invite tyranny. They are traitors to democracy and have no reason to complain when their leaders bungle them into senseless wars.

The just-war criteria are also the business of churches and nongovernmental organizations. In Christian terms, citizenship is a vocation and a commitment to be involved and informed. This means that many Christians are sinful citizens.[5] What follows are the tests (in reading them try applying them to American invasions of Vietnam, Grenada, Panama, Iraq, and so forth).

Criterion 1: A Just Cause

A just cause for state-sponsored violence is usually described as that which promotes justice and peace. That means that you don't start an aggressive war to get what you want (oil, more territory, or to wreak vengeance for past offenses); you go to war to defend yourself when you have no other alternatives. Defense is the only "just cause." As ethicist David Hollenbach writes: "The only *just cause* is defense against unjust attack."[6] Aggressive or preemptive wars simply open the door to international barbarism.

Obviously, preventive or preemptive war (a handy disguise for aggressive war) is immoral and unjust by this criterion since it sets out to prevent future dangers by attacking any *imagined* enemies. It would sanction attacks on anyone we imagined might someday, somehow, be a threat to us. It is the logic of a bully. It is no surprise that Colin Powell was chosen as secretary of state by President Bush. In 1992 testimony to the House Armed Services Committee, he stated it bluntly: "I want to be the bully on the block." For this country he wanted "sufficient power . . . to deter any challenger from ever dreaming of challenging us on the world stage."[7] Bullies do not wait for "a just cause." They don't wait for an attack. Bullies are preemptive. Understandably, people don't like them.

The current "National Security Strategy of the United States" is a bully policy. As George W. Bush explained it, "We must confront the worst threats before they emerge."[8] This amounts to a "shoot first, ask questions later" policy. The National Security Strategy announced that "we will not hesitate to act alone" (thus violating the U.N. Charter to which we are bound by treaty to respond to threats collectively) and that we will not hesitate to act "preemptively."[9]

That puts the United States shamefully in Hitler's camp, since the Nuremberg trials treated his preemptive war as a war crime.[10] It also violates one of the still-relevant aspects of the Treaty of Westphalia in 1648, which insisted on noninterference by one state in the internal affairs of another.[11] Ironically, as the first president in American history to be fighting and losing two wars simultaneously (Iraq and Afghanistan, misadventures that do not admit of "victory"), George W. Bush may be providing tragic proof of the cruel folly of "preemptive war."

Preemptive war, of course, is the prime tool of empire. Empire is the control of weaker nations for the advantage of the imperial nation, and you can't build an empire without preemptive and aggressive war. The United Sates has been empire building since it first drove the Native Americans off lands they had occupied for

thousands of years. We then started an aggressive war to seize from Mexico what is now
Texas, New Mexico, Arizona, Utah, Nevada,
California, and parts of Colorado. From Spain
we then, again by war, acquired land in the
Caribbean and the Philippines. Later we took
Hawaii. Our need for empire continues. We
have eight hundred military installations in
130 countries and our Special Forces operate
in nearly 170 nations. We spend more on the
military than the next eighteen largest nations
combined. If nations won't let us in, we invade
them militarily or we tell them we'll boycott
them out of our market. We take up 20 percent
of Okinawa's arable land for our bases; and if
the Japanese protest, they are threatened with
being denied access to our markets. We have
overthrown some twenty governments in the
last century, but would take a dim view if any
nation tried to overthrow ours.[12]

Empire builders do not scruple about "just
causes." A "just cause" according to the Charter
of the United Nations exists when we (or others)
are under attack and we react defensively in
cooperation with the other nations of the U.N.
To be "just," war must be truly defensive in this
sense. This is also the criterion of the just-war
theory. The goal is to impose some restraints
on vengeance, greed, and the other passions
of war and to encourage peaceful negotiations
and deal-making without shedding blood.

Criterion 2: Declaration by Competent Authority

The reason for this criterion is that war can be moral only if it is an action to protect the common good. *Government, by definition, is the prime caretaker of the common good.* A nation cannot be committed to war by private interests (even though this is what actually often happens when oil interests or the interests of corporations are the real but hidden motive for an attack).[13]

In a democracy, the government is supposed to represent the people. It is naïve to think it always does so. Power tends to fall into the hands of a few. Shrinking the *we* in "we the people" is the constant temptation to tyranny in a democracy. Decisions are made not by the people *en masse* but by a small number of people who hold effective power. In the important matter of war, the framers of our Constitution tried to democratize the decision as much as possible so that it would represent as many of the people as possible.

Article One, Section 8 of the U.S. Constitution says that it is the prerogative of Congress "to declare war" and to "provide for the common Defence." Moreover, it gives Congress the power to provide the money for war and to cut off that money if it does not approve of the way the war is being conducted. James Madison said that "in no part of the Constitution is more wisdom to be found than in the clause which confides the question of war and peace to the legislature and not to the executive department."[14]

This wise provision of the Constitution has been dismissed by American presidents and Congress ever since the Korean War. President Harry S. Truman began the trashing by going to war without the required declaration by Congress. Interestingly, however, this failure was noted at the time; more recently we simply ignore the Constitution without comment. The Senate went along with the president but "it did not want to declare war and enlarge" the president's powers.[15] There was a recognition that they were giving rights to the president and that these rights were limited because it was an undeclared war. Since that time, this concern for the Constitution has been dropped, and all American wars have been undeclared and, therefore, illegal.

Since that time, the Constitution has been violated with the consent of the Congress and the American people, including all of those who call for "strict constructionism" in interpreting the Constitution. Instead, at most, Congress votes on vague resolutions allowing the president to do whatever he pleases whenever he chooses. It gives the president dictatorial power. Thus, President Johnson, after a falsified report on a Tonkin Bay incident, was given the power to go to war as he saw fit. The House of Representatives voted for this unanimously and only two senators voted against it.[16] The Supreme Court was asked to declare this war unconstitutional and it repeatedly declined to do so. A cowardly Congress (backed by an indolent and indifferent citizenry and judiciary) handed over their constitutional rights to the president. The debacle of Vietnam followed.

A timid Congress did the same for George W. Bush after the attacks on September 11, 2001.[17] All of this moves the presidency toward monarchy and dishonors the founders of the nation who struggled heroically to move us from monarchy to a constitutional democracy.

Inert citizens who sit by and let this happen with nary a whimper of protest are as guilty as their leaders. Anne Frank wrote in her diary: "I don't believe that only governments and capitalists are guilty of aggression. Oh no, the little man is just as keen on it, for otherwise the people of the world would have risen in revolt long ago."[18]

Some would say that this need for a declaration of war is no longer feasible since modern war often involves a battle with a nonstate entity such as Al-Qaeda and the just-war theory supposes state actors. Even today, however, states are the ones that react and target those whom they call "terrorists." And when these states act, they inevitably enter the territory of another state. Israel enters the Palestinian territory to bomb and raze houses; Russia goes into Afghanistan and Chechnya; and, of course, the United States invades or bombs other nations whenever it decides that "terrorists" are there. The need for proper declaration of war is a hedge against vigilantism. This part of the just-war theory remains relevant and dishonored.

The fact is that this declaration-of-war provision is practical as well as moral. The United States has started a streak of losing wars. We lost in Vietnam and are mired in Afghanistan and Iraq, not a good record for a supposed "superpower." Why this string of losses? As Yale professor of international relations Bruce Russett says, democracies "more often win their wars—80 percent of the time." The reason is "they are more prudent about what wars they get into, choosing wars that they are more likely to win and that will incur lower costs." "The more democratic states are, the more peaceful their relations are likely to be."[19] None of these three losing misadventures—Vietnam, Iraq, Afghanistan—could be called "prudent." None were declared according to the Constitution, which demands prudence. One reason we are losing wars is because we now go to war like autocracies, not like democracies.

But what about revolutions? Much has been written about the justifiability of violent revolutions against corrupt governments that have lost all legitimacy in the eyes of the people. It is more difficult to justify violence of this sort since the possibilities for chaos are greater. Who among the revolutionaries would have the authority to declare a war? If a government has lost all legitimacy, a revolution could only be instigated, when *all* nonviolent means of resistance have been exhausted and when sufficient legitimacy attaches to an emerging authority. There is abundant evidence, as we will see below, of successful nonviolent revolutions; indeed, there is a strong moral bias, *and even a strategic bias*, in favor of the nonviolent revolution and against violent revolution.

Criterion 3: Right Intention

This criterion asks the *why* and the *how* questions. It focuses on both *jus ad bellum*, the decision to go to war, and *jus in bello*, the actual conduct of the war. The *why* question is critical. Proclaimed good intentions are the refuge of scoundrels. Always presume a divide between a nation's *announced intention* and its *real motives*. As governments see it, candor is not the best policy when trying to rally a nation to the enormous exertions of war.

Knowing why we turn to the slaughter of war is crucial since, when wars start, examination of conscience seems increasingly unpatriotic, replaced by mindless calls to "support our troops" no matter what the poor troops are being sent to do.[20] Here, spelled out with an

eye to realistic peacemaking, are the requirements for "right intention."

A. "Right intention" insists that the "just
cause" you allege for going to war is really
why you are going to war. Citizens and the
press should never be more alert and vocal
than when their government is about to go
out and kill people in their name. Wars begin
in a fog of lies called propaganda. Intelligent
citizens should know that the alleged reasons
for a war bear a huge burden of proof. In his
study of violence, René Girard says that "foreign wars" are often waged to divert us from
internal problems that threaten "the cohesion"
of the nation. So we strike out at others to
avoid fixing the problems we have at home.[21]

War is also rooted in our most primitive
instinct of vengeance. The Russian philosopher
Nicholas Berdyaev says that "vengeance is the
chief moral emotion of ancient humanity."[22]
Ancient peoples often believed that only by the
shedding of blood could the debt incurred by
certain crimes be satisfied. This was the meaning of the Jewish *go'el* and the Arab *tar.* "The
blood of a kinsman must be avenged by the
death of the one who shed it, or, failing him,
by the blood of one of his family."[23] Despite
the lofty, euphemistic rhetoric that accompa-
nies the start of war, the reality is often (as in
capital punishment) a brutal and irrational lust
for vengeance. Such motivation violates "right
intention."

Excessive secrecy during war is commonplace and a violation of "right intention." Governmental secrecy in wartime often is a means of control. It is not maintained because "loose lips sink ships" (often the enemy already knows the secret); it is a tactic to keep the people in the dark and, thus, compliant with the war makers. It is the *vox populi* that is feared. The goal is preventing dissent, not attacks. This, of course, denies citizens any role in the decision for war. Democracy is one of the first sacrifices demanded by the god of war.

The desire of a government committed to the multiple demands of war-making is to reduce citizens to flag wavers. This disenfranchises citizens, banishing them from the determination of "right intention" and making the "commander in chief" a *de facto* dictator. As anthropologist Ernest Becker points out, democracy was based on the idea that leaders need to be curbed because they will otherwise be "corrupted by power into making decisions that are self-defeating."[24] It was this idea that motivated the American Revolution and the founding of this republic. The challenge for any democracy, as philosopher Karl Popper says, is to get citizens so activated "that bad or incompetent rulers can be prevented from doing too much damage."[25] Certainly in the United States, flaccid citizens are not fulfilling this duty.

The all-too-common sin of citizens is defection. They become passive pawns, putty in the leader's hands. And the leader has great tools to do this. Religion is one of them. National-ism elicits religious fervor. Economic histo-rian Arnold Toynbee goes so far as to say that "nationalism is 90 percent of the religion of 90 percent of the people of the Western World and of the rest of the World as well."[26] So people may call themselves Christians or Jews, but their religious ardor is fixed on the nation. They will die for it and honor those who do and they will pay taxes without demur for any quixotic adventure on which the government embarks. As Old Testament scholar Norman Gottwald notes, "Blasphemy and treason are closely connected" in human history. To attack or even disagree with the government "is to dishonor and disobey the gods."[27] Leaders know this instinctively and use it. After September 11, 2001, a White House spokesman noted that the president "considers any opposition to his poli-cies to be no less than an act of treason."[28]

The real treason after 9/11 was commit-ted by Congress, which, during the "week of shame," October 3 to 10, voted in both houses to give to the president the war-making power the Constitution had consigned to them. Flag-waving citizens were complicit in this treason and share the shame.

Since Jesus died fighting tyranny, Chris-tians should be the last to join the worship of a warrior-king. On the contrary, they too often join the chorus of blind obedience, allowing private piety to free them from the hard work of prophetic citizenry.

"Right intention" also brings us to the prime victims of war, the soldiers who are sent to fight it. Modern war requires that soldiers be regimented into a slavish docility. The training of soldiers and all the martial rituals do not produce the swashbuckling knights of yore but rigid, salute-on-demand automatons. Any other response is judged and treated as criminal. Thus, those closest to the war are denied any role in testing the rightness of "right intention."

The need for regimentation of soldiers is obvious. Healthy people do not have a proclivity to slaughter. Basic training is designed to train a nonviolent person into someone who is a willing killer of other people. Some cultures make this clear. "The young Scandinavian had to become a bear before he could become an elite warrior, going 'berserk' (the word means 'dressed in a bear hide'), biting and chasing people."[29] Other cultures use drugs and hallucinogens to rev up soldiers for battle and then put them through various rituals after the battle to make them normal again. Though we do not dress our warriors in face paint or bearskin (our preference is khaki), we do mark them out as different. The serious psychological problems soldiers suffer after returning from war (post-traumatic stress disorder) testifies to how violent it is to force people to be violent.

B. "Right intention" means that war is only justified if it serves justice and eventual peace. Any other intention is not "right." The American Catholic Bishops point out that if you impose unnecessary conditions like "unconditional surrender" (a demand that needlessly extended World War II), your intention is not "right."[30] Unrealistic demands show vindictiveness, not a hunger for justice and peace. Right intention means that justice and peace, not the humiliation of your enemies—or access to their oil—is your real, truly intended goal. Obviously, torture of prisoners in your control undermines any claims of a "right intention."

Whether a nation has a "right intention" appears up in bold relief in the way it concludes a war. World War I was concluded in such a way as to make World War II predictable and predicted. Germany was saddled with unmanageable demands for "reparations" on the basis that it was 100 percent responsible for the war—an absurd presumption since nations and their policies are never immaculately conceived. It was also established at the Treaty of Versailles that Germany and the Allies would both disarm. The Allies did not, however, and thus the stage was set for the rise of Adolf Hitler, who concluded, like Napoleon, that Europe needed one hegemonic power for stability—the same thinking that motivates the American empire today.[31]

Assessing "right intention," when it comes to what theologian Reinhold Niebuhr called "the feeble mind of a nation," is a challenge. Part of a nation's feeble-mindedness is in memory loss. The attack on Pearl Harbor was criminal, but it is simplistically seen as an unprovoked atrocity, a "day of infamy," with us cast as the innocent victims. Prior to the attack, however, we and our allies had been aggressively squeezing Japan economically. "Economic pressure on Japan commenced with the freezing of Japanese assets in the United States as early as *July 25, 1941*."[32] More trade restrictions were applied as late as December 2, 1941, five days before Pearl Harbor. Japan had been cut off from as much as 25 percent of its normal imports. Nations are amnesiacs when explaining how they got into trouble—all the more reason to probe their alleged "right intentions."

C. "Right intention" also means that a nation does not go to war and put most of the burdens for that war on some people while sparing others. It means, that since war waged by a state is an act of a political community, the burdens should be shared fairly throughout the community. When there is no military draft, as is now the case in the United States, it is most often the children of the poor, not the children of the rich who go to war. We now field an army of people, many of whom joined seeking a way out of poverty or to get an education. The situation more and more resembles an army of mercenaries since even bonuses are offered to get enlistments. Putting a "Support our Troops" sticker on the back of one's SUV does not support the troops or share their plight or their risks. If anything, it is a cynical badge of indifference.

This class-based tendency for fielding armies of the poor is not new. At the time of the Revolutionary War, "the rich, it turned out, could avoid the draft by paying for substitutes; the poor had to serve . . . the military became a place of promise for the poor, who might rise in rank, acquire some money, change their social status."[33] The same was true at the time of the Civil War. As Howard Zinn writes: the wealthy "[J. P.] Morgan had escaped military service in the Civil War by paying $300.00 to a substitute. So did John D. Rockefeller, Andrew Carnegie, Philip Armour, Joy Gould, and James Mellon. Mellon's father had written to him that 'a man may be a patriot without risking his own life or sacrificing his health. There are plenty of lives less valuable.'"[34]

This is the thinking of the upper class. Vice President Dick Cheney got five deferments from the draft during the Vietnam invasion, alleging "other priorities." It is not surprising that this could be arranged since, as historian Richard Hofstadter says, the United States has always been "a middle class society governed for the most part by its upper classes."[35] The amazing thing is how the lower classes go along with this: they will die sooner than challenge this arrangement.

The modern American economy has made it possible to make war painless for the vast majority of citizens so as to maintain passive support for the war. As historian David Kennedy writes, today "thanks to something [called] the 'revolution in military affairs,' . . . we now have an active-duty military establishment that is, proportionate to population, about 4 percent of the size of the force that won World War II. . . . And today's military budget is about 4 percent of gross domestic product, as opposed to nearly 40 percent during World War II."[36] For most of the population the "bread and circus" show goes on, their daily comforts are not disturbed, and this puts their consciences into a stupor. Of course, all will suffer eventually as the treasuries are drained by the war-makers, but for a time it quells resistance.

So the formula for current U.S. autocratic war-making is simple: an indifferent public, a somnambulant press, religious people distracted by issues like same-sex marriages and abortion, a group of ruthless ideologues in high office—and three lost wars in a row.

Having a right intention with all it implies would spare us all of that. Morality, after all, is practical.

D. "Right intention" also means that if you cannot "love your enemies" you will at least try to understand them and their grievances.

If you would kill them without trying with an open and fair mind to understand their wrath, you are neither just nor smart. If you declare them worthy of death but not of understanding, your intention is not "right." If racism enters into your "image of the enemy," your intention is even more polluted. If you can speak of "Palestinian terrorism" but have nothing to say to the Palestinians who hold deeds to homes from which they were forcibly expelled, your focus is narrow and your intention is not "right." You should be able to speak of both. If you can condemn the suicide attacks of 9/11 but have no interest in exploring why people hate us so much they will kill themselves to kill us, your intention is morally flawed.

Criterion 4:
The Principle of Discrimination and Noncombatant Immunity

This is a bedrock principle of just-war theory. This means that you may never directly, intentionally target noncombatants, that is, innocent civilians. The modern science of war puts this principle under major stress. This well-intentioned restraint is hardly possible in modern warfare. When knights charged one another in an open field, the noncombatants could be bystanders. The history and science of war have changed that.

Also, this principle implies that it is always legitimate to kill combatants (soldiers) who are presumed guilty of death even though they may be reluctant civilians forced into uniform. Furthermore, with advances in the science of weaponry, how do you go after combatants only? Science has all but eliminated a safe zone for civilians. "In the wars of the 1990s, civilian deaths constituted between 75 and 90 percent of all war deaths."[37] In war also, efforts are made to deny food, fuel, and medicine to enemy forces. But how can a distinction be made between military food and civilian food? Unless noncombatants are moved to another part of the planet, modern war will find them and punish them. From land mines to nuclear weapons, civilians can't escape the multiple "ground zeros" of modern war.

To target civilians intentionally, of course, is *terrorism*. By definition, *terrorism is an attack on civilians as a way of getting a response from their leaders*. Terrorism is immoral whether done by individual suicide bombers or by "shock-and-awe" invading armies or by Israeli missile attacks on crowded Palestinian settlement camps. When it comes to terrorism, state terrorists are the worst offenders.

The science of war with its increased powers of obliteration has trumped the moral hopes of the principle of discrimination and noncombatant immunity. This new fact of indiscriminate weaponry adds massively to the burden of proof when a modern nation decides on the violence of war as its policy. The cost of maintaining this massive kill-power means that killing, not humanitarian aid and eco-logical concern, are our budgetary preference. It means that our foreign policy is ultimately based on violence and the threat of violence, not in making friends by bringing help and healing to populations and nations in need.

Here is a significant fact, unknown to most Americans: of the twenty-two richest nations of the world, we are first in wealth and last in developmental assistance; among those richest nations we are the stingiest. The United States' percentage of national income to humanitar-ian assistance is embarrassingly low compared to nearly any other developed nation—we give less that one-tenth of one percent (.1 percent), compared to .97 percent for the Danes, .89 percent for the Swedes, .55 percent for the French, and .31 percent for the Germans. Even in absolute terms, if we exclude U.S. aid to Israel and Egypt (which is largely military aid used in Israel to occupy and oppress Palestin-ians and in Egypt to suppress democracy, mak-ing neither Israel or Egypt or the world more secure), the United States—with 300 million people—spends less on development assistance than Denmark, a nation of five million.[38] Bud-gets are moral documents. They show where your heart is. In their own way, they can be a form of violence.

Teachers of Terrorism

The classical examples of deliberate terrorism (and violations of the principle of discrimination) were the atomic bombings of Hiroshima and Nagasaki. General Marshall urged that we give a warning to the civilians to get out so that only military targets could be hit. He was ignored. Terror was now official United States policy. The purpose of atomic terror bombing was to force the Japanese leaders to surrender unconditionally. It seemed to have worked. (Terror often does, at least for awhile. Then it tends to blow back at you.) However, the United States Strategic Bombing Survey set up by the War Department in 1944 concluded that Japan was already defeated and "would have surrendered even if the atomic bombs had not been dropped."[39] Some think the purpose of the bombing was to "send a message" to the Soviet Union; in other words, killing Japanese people to send a message to Russian leaders—atomic holocaust as a means of communication![40]

In private life, where morality is more monitored and regulated, killing someone to send a message to someone else is murder. When we act collectively we are more morally obtuse.

It is, of course, no slight irony that the United States, a self-declared leader in a "war on terror," is the only nation to have used weapons of mass destruction in acts of terrorism against civilian populations. Of course, we were well-practiced terrorists before we dropped the atomic bombs. As Michael Walzer points out, terrorism "became a feature of conventional war" in World War II.[41] Following our example, it also became then a tactic of revolutionary and insurgency wars thereafter. We and our allies led the way and now we are the self-righteous denouncers of terrorism.

Terror was the explicit policy of the Allies in World War II. Winston Churchill noted that "the severe, ruthless bombing of Germany on an ever-increasing scale will not only cripple her war effort . . . but will create conditions intolerable to the mass of the German population."[42]

Churchill, in belated scruple, worried as the war moved on if bombing civilian centers "simply for the sake of increasing the terror" was something that should be "reviewed." He didn't worry enough. It was not reviewed and the terror was practiced until the end of the war. Up to 100,000 people died in bombings such as that of Dresden and Tokyo, and huge numbers of men, women, and children died in the holocausts of Hamburg, Berlin, and other cities. "The civilian death toll from Allied terrorism in World War II must have exceeded half a million men, women, and children."[43]

When the Germans practiced this form of terrorist bombing in Rotterdam and Coventry and elsewhere, Franklin D. Roosevelt described it as "inhuman barbarism that has profoundly shocked the conscience of humanity."[44] The psychology of war shows that moral shock is an early casualty in war. We imitate our enemies and they imitate us in a race to the moral bottom.

Conscience Tremors

Pathological killers are not the norm. And yet war requires a dulling of conscience to make killing seem good and even heroic and patriotic. Consciences talk back, however, especially when it comes to killing civilians. The inherent stresses of the just-war theory show up in the strained efforts to keep the killing within some bounds. This is understandable since, *if "war" is not "just," it is a massacre.* If noncombatants are not immune, it is a massacre. The tortured efforts to enforce it may suggest that in practice the rules are functioning mainly as a rationalization for mayhem.

Some examples illustrate the contorted efforts at concern for noncombatants. In ancient India, the law said that the following people should be spared any harm in war. Exempted from violence are: "those who look on without taking part, those afflicted with grief, those who are asleep, thirsty, or fatigued or are walking along the road, or have a task on hand unfinished, or who are proficient in fine art."[45] One senses that this would present challenges to an army on the move. The list does not do well in a reality check. It shows a frantic, almost comical, effort to minimize the horror.

Sieges, of course, lump soldiers and civilians together in peril but they have always been a part of war. "More civilians died in the siege of Leningrad than in the infernos of Hamburg, Dresden, Tokyo, Hiroshima and Nagasaki taken together."[46] The Talmud tried to minimize the damage of war with a curious suggestion, summarized by Maimonides in the twelfth century: "When siege is laid to a city for the purposes of capture, it may not be surrounded on all four sides, but only on three, in order to give an opportunity for escape to those who would flee to save their lives." Grotius in the seventeenth century related the same idea. The idea, of course, as Michael Walzer says, is "hopelessly naïve."[47] A siege with an open side is not a siege. Those making rules for war easily plunge into self-contradiction.

With wars and massacres raging in the tenth century in Europe, the bishops tried to put limits on the violence. They instituted rules known as "the Truce of God." The first rules banned all killing during the forty days of Lent and for several weeks thereafter. Killing was also to be avoided during the four weeks before Christmas, on all Fridays, Sundays, and holy days—of which there were many. (One needed a keen sense of time and a reliable calendar to know when killing might commence.) Church properties and the clergy were always to be exempt from violence. (The clergy were, after all, writing these rules.) Also immune to violence were peasants and pilgrims, agricultural animals, and olive trees. From age twelve on, everyone was bound to take an oath to obey these rules and, with revealing irony, to kill any who would not conform.[48]

One of these oaths comes down to us from Robert the Pious. We can see a definite lapse from the rigors of the rules just cited. This Robert, who merited the encomium "pious" (suggesting he was a cut above his peers), displayed a keen talent for tactical distinctions: "I will not burn houses or destroy them, unless there is a knight inside. I will not root up vines. I will not attack noble ladies, nor their maids nor widows or nuns, unless it is their fault. From the beginning of Lent to the end of Easter I will not attack an unarmed Knight."[49] The Truce of God was an effort to treat the disease of war. The comment of Stanley Windass rings true: "The disease was too radical to respond to such first aid."[50] Indeed, the rules come across as a kind of desperate pleading. They often do little more than put in bold relief the horror they are trying to regulate, the horror that it is our moral duty to avoid with all the genius we can muster.

In spite of the best efforts of rule-makers, war tends to become "a circus of slaughter."

If one side breaks a rule, the other is strategically disadvantaged by not breaking it. Thus, all restraints are fragile and the need to prevent the situation (war) where restraints are so fragile is a supreme moral obligation, one that must burden the consciences of citizens and not just their leaders.

Nuclear War

Nuclear war is clearly banned by the principle of discrimination and noncombatant immunity. The prospect of such war in a world where these weapons are proliferating led the bishops of the Second Vatican Council to this blunt statement: "Any act of war aimed indiscriminately at the destruction of entire cities or of extensive areas along with their population is a crime against God and humanity itself. It merits unequivocal and unhesitating condemnation."[51] Military strategists seem to concede this when they introduce the concept of a "limited nuclear war." This is both disingenuous and wickedly naïve. Once the move from "conventional" to "unconventional" has been made, there would be no reasonable expectation that restraint by those attacked would be the sequel. There are many "weapons of mass destruction" available on the open weapons market today (chemical and biological, as well as nuclear), and many conventional weapons used *en masse* could have comparable effects.

Small atomic weapons of suitcase size can be brought anywhere and detonated. Those doing so in response to a "limited nuclear attack" could say that their response is also "limited."

What expectation is there that a nation made the target of even a so-called limited nuclear attack would not avail itself of every weapon available? With the use of any nuclear weapon, a critical threshold would be crossed. Even slight familiarity with the psychology and history of war confirms the deluge that would follow.

For this reason the only moral approach to nuclear weapons is to begin disarmament since they have no reasonable or moral use. It is strange to the point of weird to see the major holder of nuclear weapons, the only nation to have used such weapons on population centers, self-righteously ordering other nations not to develop such weapons. It is like the village sot preaching sobriety while drunk. It can hardly be convincing. In reality, American use of and maintenance of such weapons has made these weapons the coin of the realm. Nations like North Korea have demonstrated that even the claim to having them protects them from attack. If it were known that Iraq had such weapons and the ability to deliver them, it would not have been invaded.

American preaching for nuclear sobriety is also undercut by our support of Israel's possession of atomic weapons. We not only tolerate this but even finance it with our tax dollars. Israel's neighbors have noticed this, as has the rest of the world. It is a motive for proliferation.

When Theory Bends

Theory is often a mask. We do something and then we find a theory to justify it. It is not only warriors who tend to go berserk in war; conspiring theorists follow them down the war-greased slide. Barbara Ehrenreich, in her brilliant book *Blood Rites: Origins and History of the Passions of War*, observes that when war is entered on, there is a burst of enthusiasm. It takes on religious fervor. Suddenly, "totems representative of the collectivity" appear; "sacred images" such as "yellow ribbons and flags" are unfurled in abundance. Everyone can get caught in this social trance. At the outbreak of World War I, even the young Mohandas Gandhi recruited his countrymen to join the British army. Sigmund Freud joined in the frenzy, confessing that he had given "all his libido to Austria-Hungary." Arnold Toynbee was so captured by it all that he produced several volumes of "atrocity propaganda" as his contribution to the war effort.[52] After the U.S. invasion of Panama in 1989, President George H. W. Bush was credited in the *New York Times* for having succeeded in an "initiation rite" by showing his "willingness to shed blood."[53]

Germans speak of *Siegentrunkenheit*, that is, getting drunk on war. Obviously, war fulfills many needs in the human psyche, creating a sense of unity that peacetime rarely can. It offers a rewarding immersion in a cause that is greater than yourself. It stirs many of the emotions found at sports events. If only something like "the kind of sharing that would end all poverty" could stir similar passions, there would be no poor people in the world. All the more reason to be slow to start a war, since we go there half-cocked and nearly mad. Moral refinements like sparing noncombatants are no match for this gripping temporary mania. This has led some philosophers such as David Hume to say that "the rage and violence of public war" brings about "a suspension of justice among the warring parties."[54]

In fact, however, the warring parties and those who write about the "rules of war" do not want to say they are suspending justice. Instead, they proclaim principles to make war "just" but then, under claims of so-called military necessity, they bend to make the most extraordinary exceptions to those principles. Francesco de Vitoria, a Spanish priest and theologian, writing in the sixteenth century, said soldiers need not know—in fact, they should not know—whether the killing they are doing is moral or immoral. If the prince had to answer such questions, "the state would fall into great peril."[55] This, in effect, depersonalizes soldiers, lifting them out of the moral realm and saying they should operate like machines without conscience. A remarkable concession for a moralist writing on "the law of war"! Vitoria also allows for sack and pillage by soldiers if it is "necessary for the conduct of the war . . . as a spur to the courage of the troops."[56] Since sack and pillage usually involve rape, this is no slight allowance. Again, the madness of state-sponsored violence seeps into theory and blesses many horrors.

Beating the Rap through the Principle of Double Effect

This double-effect principle has been called, somewhat pompously but accurately, the principle of psychological and moral disassociation. It merits attention here because it is regularly used by warriors, even by those who know nothing of its theoretical development.

The core insight of the principle is simple enough. We often do good things that have bad effects. So, we remove a cancerous uterus: there are two effects, one good (the cancer is gone), one bad (the woman is infertile). So the principle of double effect sought to answer the question, Am I morally responsible for that bad effect? The answer is, "No, as long as you did not really *want* that bad effect and as long as there was *proportionality* between the effects." That's the gist of this much-used and much-abused principle.[57]

In war, the "good effect" (doing something to defeat the enemy) drowns out even the most horrific "bad effects." Somehow it is supposed to be possible to will the good effect (the weakening of the enemy) and merely permit and tolerate the unfortunate bad effects (for instance, deaths of one hundred thousand people in Tokyo or Dresden). Today, anything that might "defeat terrorism" is justified, including our own terrorism. This is the trickery that comes into the use of double-effect thinking in wartime.

Some stunning examples: in his four-volume study on *Moral and Pastoral Theology*, Father Henry Davis, S.J., justifies starving a population by blockade or siege. As Davis puts it, "Enemy troops may be starved by blockade. If civilians suffer, it is not intended that they should suffer; it is their misfortune, and it is due to the fortune of a just war that they happen to be in the same place as their army. Blockade and siege are in principle not different from the bombing of fortified garrison towns."[58] Note that this quote is from the 1949 edition of Davis's book. Note, too, that a few years before, more civilians died in the siege of Leningrad than in the infernos of Hamburg, Dresden, Tokyo, Hiroshima, and Nagasaki taken together. Father Davis's words? "It is their misfortune." Cold comfort indeed.

Here is another example of how, when one thinks of war as inevitable and normal, conclusions are reached to go where even warriors shy to venture. Father Davis talks about bombing "hospital ships with the wounded on board." It is a momentary relief to see that he first of all rejects this. But, wait—he is not finished. "The case may be imagined when even a hospital ship will be so valuable to the enemy for future aggression during a war that it may be of vital concern to sink it. Though such a necessity would be deplorable, we think the sinking of it may be justified, for what is attacked is the ship, the deaths of those on board are incidental and not wished."[59]

Writing four years after the Hiroshima and Nagasaki bombings he says: "The morality of the use in war of the atomic bomb is not different from the morality of the use of any other explosive."[60]

This is double effect at its worst. It imagines that one could bomb a hospital ship full of the wounded and that you would not be willing their deaths. You are only willing the destruction of the ship that *may* some day be used for aggressive purposes. The slaughter you are doing is not "willed," not "intended," only "permitted." You are psychologically and morally off the hook. This is hairsplitting at its silliest. It does illustrate, however, how theory can be polluted by our long history of thinking war as just another part of politics. When push comes to shove, Clausewitz tends to win—that is, war is normal, just another way for nations to do their business.

Father Davis should have taken instruction from a fellow Jesuit moralist, John Ford. Ford wrote an article in 1944 on "The Morality of Obliteration Bombing" at the very time such bombing was going on, which he condemned. He did so, making sensitive use of—of all things—the "principle of double effect." Ford argued that it was impossible for bombardiers to drop bombs and somehow not intend to kill the people on the ground. You cannot drop your bombs and withhold your intention to have those bombs do what they will inevitably do. No "military necessity" is proportionate to the slaughter you wreak. Following Father Ford's same line of thinking, the Vatican Council condemned the view that you could view atomic weapons as simply another bomb. The use of it merits, they said, "unequivocal and unhesitating condemnation."

Ecological concerns must also be taken into account in applying the "principle of discrimination." The atomic bombs of 1945 were properly seen as cutting history in two: *the prior time*, when nature could recover from the greatest wounds we inflicted, and *now*, when we can inflict wounds that nature cannot heal. Many of our weapons and ingredients in our weapons can now leave parts of the biosphere damaged for the indefinite future or even permanently.

War has a way of making cowards of conscience. With all the struggling and stretching to keep a moral focus, even the well-intentioned easily buckle. "Military necessity" prevails. As one Protestant scholar observed in 1950: "Christian conscience in wartime seems to have chiefly the effect . . . of making Christians do reluctantly what military necessity requires."[61] And not just Christians. Therein lies our obligation, if saved our species will be, to get the "normal" out of war, to build walls of assumptions against it, and to arouse our dormant genius to build a viable ethics of peace.

Now to the last two tests to distinguish a just from an unjust war—and the very number of these requirements shows how agonizing was the effort to tame the monster which is state-sponsored violence.

Criteria 5 and 6: Last Resort and the Principle of Proportionality

These two criteria are relevant both to the decision to go to war (*jus ad bellum*) and to the means used in the war (*jus in bello*). The bloated military budget of the United States shows that war is not seen as a "last resort." Rather, the use or permanent threat of military violence ranks high in our policy options. Things like diplomacy and generous and intelligently targeted foreign aid of the sort that helps people and wins friends—these options are underfunded. This is a bellicose, chip-on-shoulder posture. It shows none of the reluctance to go violent that is the hallmark of the civilized. It shows no awareness that *coopera-tion in an interdependent, shrinking, and eco-logically crumbling world is the only wisdom.*

The "last-resort" principle is simple: *resort-ing to violence when there are neglected alter-natives is barbaric.* If state-sponsored violence is not our very last resort, we stand morally with hoodlums who would solve problems by murder.

"The principle of proportionality" has been described this way: "the damage to be inflicted and the costs incurred by war must be pro-portionate to the good expected by taking up arms."[62] More simply, the violence of war must do more good than harm. As weapons grow, wars are less and less able to pass this test.

War is a massive expedition of destruction. It is no easy thing to set up a scale to measure the good versus the evil done in such explosive events. The principle of proportionality says we have to try because if we are doing more harm than good, our killing is wrong and murderous. Political scientist William V. O'Brien points out that "the balance sheet of good and evil" must not include only the warring parties. "Inter-national interdependence means that interna-tional conflicts are difficult to contain and that their shock waves affect third parties in a man-ner that must be accounted for in the calculus of probable good and evil."[63] Binges of violence lead to hangovers. The atomic bombing of Hiroshima and Nagasaki are defended as the quick fix that ended the war. The consequence: we introduced a new weapon and started the nuclear arms race.

In judging proportionality, we must weigh the fact that war begets war. Each war sends the message that when push comes to shove, this is the way to get things done. Any nation that relies on war puts others in the position of having to reply in kind, or at least be ready to. Some nations resist that. Sweden has not been in a war in two hundred years, even though it lives in a dangerous neighborhood. Its weapons are all defensive and can threaten no one, but Sweden and Costa Rica (which has no army) are exceptions. In general, war-making makes more wars by a kind of "epidemicity."[64] As René Girard writes, "Violence is self-propagating. Everyone wants to strike the last blow, and reprisal can thus follow reprisal without any true conclusion ever being reached."[65]

In the challenging calculus of good versus evil in war, we cannot overlook what being ready for war does to shape economies. Karl Marx saw how the "means of production" shape societies; Barbara Ehrenreich notes that "the means of destruction" do so also.[66] As we have seen above, war spending squashes social spending, aircraft carriers triumph over schools and health care.

A good criterion of morality in any context—and certainly in questions of war—is this: *what is good for kids is good; what is bad for kids is ungodly.*[67] This elementary ethical principle applies saliently to war. War today cannot spare children. In weighing proportionality, what is a higher value than children? This alone builds mountains of presumptions against the military option.

War may be moral if placed in the context of law and collective action envisioned by the United Nations Charter, but even this war is full of disasters. It is lethal to men and women, babies and fetuses, puppies, cows, and roses. No bombs are smart when people are in the target area. And yet our species is addicted to this disaster to the point where nations define their power in terms of their capacity to kill.

The danger of the just-war theory and even of the United Nations Charter is that it may serve to suck us into the shrunken "logic of war" that treats war as normal and unavoidable. By using these tools rigidly, however, we can build a case against what the Charter calls "the scourge of war" and pry open the door to other modes of conflict resolution. When the Charter and the just-war principles are used loosely and cynically, they do serve only to rationalize the horror of war and enshrine it with unearned moral dignity. However, as the ancients said: *abusus non tollit usum*—"because something *can* be abused does not mean it cannot be intelligently used." Of course, just-war theory was abused. As religious activist Jim Wallis says: "The just war theory has been used and abused to justify far too many of our wars."[68] Religious studies professor Joseph Fahey adds, "The 'just war' model was never meant to justify war. It was meant to limit war, to control war, and even to avoid war."[69]

The peace writings of the world religions, the principles of the "just war," and instruments like the U.N. Charter are stepping stones on the way to a world without war, serious efforts to minimize the horror. Properly understood—and taken seriously—these tools build a wall against state-sponsored violence that is hard to surmount. They are to be developed and insisted on, not jettisoned as we work toward ending "the scourge of war." Properly framed and used they put the burden of proof that is now placed on the conscientious objector on the warrior .

Every war produces epics of crass rationalization and denial. We are told that Titus, the Roman emperor, when viewing the deaths his army had caused, threw "his hands up to heaven" and, calling God as his witness, he proclaimed "that it was not his doing."[70] As Michael Walzer asks, "Whose doing was it?" Donald Rumsfeld was less theatrical than Titus when the devastation of our invasion of Iraq first appeared: "Stuff happens," he shrugged. When Pope Benedict XVI visited Auschwitz, he prayed aloud: "Lord, how could you tolerate all this?"[7] The question for Titus, the pope, Rumsfeld, and all of us is, Who made "all this" happen? Wars don't *happen*. People make wars, and criteria like those of the just-war theory and the U.N. Charter call war-makers before the bar of conscience and put burdens of proof on their shoulders that should tame their truculence and weigh them down.

3

War: Is It Necessarily So?

War grips our souls like a demon. We think it natural, normal, inevitable—always regrettable, to be sure—but the ultimate guarantor of our safety and security. That's the myth that needs to be exorcized.

The Bible tried to exorcize it. Biblical people at one time were more into war than we are. The Hebrew God started out as such a ferocious warrior that he would be condemned by all the civilizing conventions formulated at Geneva, The Hague, and Nuremberg. That image of God is why the Crusaders and today's hymn "Onward Christian Soldiers" have found plenty of support in the Bible.[1] Eventually, in a remarkable breakthrough, the biblical people discovered that violent power is the most delusional and least successful. (They had their "Duh!" moment.) They saw that collective violence (war) is not intrinsic to our species and that, in fact, it is wrong. It had seemed common sense that there should always be "wars and rumors of wars," but the Israelites said, "It ain't necessarily so."

Abraham Heschel states the dramatic fact: the Israelites "were the first [people] in history to regard a nation's reliance upon force as evil."[2] They learned from experience that violence does not work; it bites back at you. As the Christian Paul put it: "If you go on fighting one another, tooth and nail, all you can expect is mutual destruction" (Gal. 5:14). So the Bible did an about-face and went on to blast military power. Its theology changed from "The LORD is a warrior" (Exod. 15:3-8) to God as "the LORD of peace" (Judg. 6:24) and the covenant, "a covenant of peace" (Isa. 54:10).

In its first three centuries, Christianity continued this critique of war until along came Constantine with a befriending sword, and the Christians buckled. They were not about to beat the friendly sword into a plowshare. The first step in this grand defection was to accommodate war using principles that grew into the just-war theory. Then in the Crusades they sacramentalized war as an instrument for the spread of God's kingdom. Bluntly put, they betrayed and still betray the peace breakthrough of the Bible.

The ancient world cynically declared what seemed to be the natural law of social evolution: *si vis pacem, para bellum* ("if you want peace, prepare for war"). In this view, in the tough world we live in, war is the only way to peace. The biblical writers entered a major dissent to this logic. They say: *si vis pacem, para pacem*—"if you want peace you have to prepare it and build it" (or, as Psalm 34:14 says, "Seek peace and pursue it"). It doesn't just happen.

It has to be built, like a city, brick by brick. But, most importantly, peace has to be seen as possible. The illusory "security through arms" heresy has to be broken.

The Israelites were practical people. They knew the meaning of power but they discovered and pioneered the idea that violent power bounces back at you. They knew that what they had learned was "a hard sell" and so they drummed this message home with passionate urgency. Their message was not always heeded; moral breakthroughs always meet resistance.

"Neither by force of arms nor by brute strength" would the people be saved (Zech. 4:6). "Not by might shall a man prevail" (1 Sam. 2:9). Military power will be discredited: "The nations shall see and be ashamed of all their might" (Mic. 7:16). "Some boast of chariots and some of horses, but our boast is the name of the LORD." Those who boast of these state-of-the-art weapons "totter and fall, but we rise up" (Ps. 20:6-7). "Their course is evil and their might is not right" (Jer. 23:10). The song of the military (usually translated as "ruthless") will be silenced, and fortified cities will become heaps of ruin (Isa. 25:5, 2). Reflecting Israel's history, the prime weapons of oppressive royalty, horses and chariots, are despised (see Exod. 14:9, 23; Deut. 20:1; 2 Sam. 15:1; 1 Kings 18:5; 22:4; 2 Kings 3:7; 18:23; 23:11). As Walter Brueggemann puts it:

"Horses and chariots are a threat to the social experiment which is Israel. . . . Yahweh is the sworn enemy of such modes of power."[3] God ordered Joshua to disarm: "Hamstring their horses and burn their chariots" (Josh. 11:6).

"There is no peace for the wicked" (Isa. 57:21). The inverse of that is that if you do not have peace, it is your fault. You took the wrong approach. "Because you have trusted in your chariots, in the number of your warriors, the tumult of war shall arise against your people and all your fortresses shall be razed" (Hos. 1:13-14). For leaders to ask their people to trust arms for deliverance is "wickedness" and "treachery" (Hos. 10:13). Arms beget fear, not peace. You cannot build "Zion in bloodshed" (Mic. 3:10). Therefore, "I will break bow and sword and weapon of war and sweep them off the earth, so that all living creatures may lie down without fear" (Hos. 2:18). Notice, the distrust of arms is seen as a norm for "all living creatures," not just for Israel. War delivers peace to no one. It's counterproductive. There is no "war to end all wars"; only peace ends war, and you have to work at peace, not just pray for it. You have to substitute justice-work for violence-waging.

Justice as the Alternative to War

The Israelites did not just criticize the *security-through-arms* illusion; they offered an alternative. Peace can only be the fruit of justice, justice for all people, not just for those in your tribe or nation. That is what the brilliant Isaiah said: *only justice "shall yield peace"* (Isa. 32:17), a text that all by itself deserves a Nobel Peace Prize. The goal of justice in Israel was the elimination of poverty: "There shall be no poor among you" (Deut. 15:4). "The poverty of the poor is their ruin," says Proverbs 10:15, and their poverty is also our undoing. You cannot build a peaceful society upon a base of poverty. That is unjust and it destroys peace. This is the biblical insight, an insight that is eternally true. Nothing coming out of the modern schools of economics rivals its brilliance. It is from the seed of justice, not from bloodshed, that peace will grow. If only "people of faith" could put aside their petty squabbles and unite around this epochal biblical insight.

The Jesus movement continued the biblical protest against kill-power as the path to security. "How blessed are the peacemakers; God shall call them his children" (Matt. 5:9).

One text, however, has muddied the Christian contribution, making it appear that Jesus was against resistance to evil. What he opposed was violent resistance, but he himself was an active nonviolent resister to empire—and it was precisely this that got him killed. (It is remarkable that his nonviolent movement survived longer than Rome.)

The misunderstood text is Matthew 5:38-42: "You have learned that they were told, 'Eye for eye, tooth for tooth.' But what I tell you is this: Do not set yourself against the man who wrongs you. If someone slaps you on the right cheek, turn and offer him your left. If a man wants to sue you for your shirt, let him have your coat as well. If a man in authority makes you go one mile, go with him two." As biblical scholar Walter Wink says, this text has been interpreted so badly that it became "the basis for systematic training in cowardice, as Christians are taught to acquiesce to evil."[4] It has been used to urge cooperation with dictators, submission to wife battering, and helpless passivity in the face of evil. Associating Jesus with such pusillanimity is an outrage.

Wink puts the meaning back into these texts. "Turn the other cheek" was not in reference to a fistfight. The reference is to an insulting, backhanded slap of a subordinate where the intention was "not to injure but to humiliate." Abject submission was the goal. Turning the other cheek was the opposite of abject submission. Rather, it said: "Try again. . . . I deny you the power to humiliate me." The striker has failed, his goal not achieved. His "inferior" is not cowering but is trivializing the insult. Gandhi the Hindu understood: "The first principle of nonviolent action is that of non-cooperation in everything humiliating."[5] This is courageous resistance, not passivity.

Similarly, the person being sued for his clothing is an example of a frequent horror in Jesus' day. The poor were strapped with debts and through debt would lose their land, their homes, and even their clothing. As Wink explains, if a man is being sued for his outer garment, he should yield it and then strip himself naked and say, "Here, take my underwear, too." Picture the victim marching out of court stark naked to the guffaws of all bystanders. And there stands the disgraced, shamed creditor holding the man's cloak and underwear. Nakedness was taboo in that society and the shame fell less on the naked party than on the person viewing or causing the nakedness (Gen. 9:20-27). This, again, was not submission, but as Wink calls it, "deft lampooning." It was nonviolent resistance.

Going the second mile: by law, the Roman occupiers could force a person to carry a soldier's heavy pack, but only for one mile. The mile limitation was a prudent ruling to minimize rebellion. There were two gains for the Roman soldier in this. He could hand over his eighty-five- to one-hundred-pound pack and gear and thus reduce the occupied person to a pack animal. But when they reached the mile marker and the soldier could be punished for forcing more than a mile, the victim could say: "Oh, no, I want to carry this for another mile." Wink tells us to imagine the situation of a Roman soldier pleading with a Jew to give him his pack back. Who's in charge now? The power has shifted.

Nonviolent resistance takes a good deal of imagination. Violence does not: even a raging bull can achieve it.

Jesus knew that violent resistance to the Roman Empire was fruitless. A similar wisdom was shown by the Danes during World War II. They did not try to fight the German army but allowed them in. Then every day their king would lead a quiet walk through the city of Copenhagen with the citizens in good order behind him. It was peaceful, but it said to the occupiers: "You do not own us and you have not captured our spirits." This had to affect even the minds of the occupiers, as nonviolent resistance always seeks to do. The same spirit showed when the Danes got word from a friendly German officer that the Germans were coming for their Jews.

Tacitus spoke for his world when he said that the gods were with the militarily mighty. Not our God, said Israel. Justice is the key to peace and security and there is no other way. That, said Israel and early Christianity, is "the way of the Lord." It is more and more obvious that it is also common sense.

But Were They Wrong?

History would seem to say that the peace dreamers of the Bible were wrong. There have been "wars and rumors of wars." This has been particularly true in the West. Robert Nisbet writes: "Whether we like it or not, the evidence is clear that for close to three thousand years, down to this very moment, Western civilization has been the single most war-ridden, war-dominated, and militaristic civilization in all human history."[6] Since 1945 there have been 135 wars, most of them in the poor world (often misnamed "developing"), and these killed more than twenty-two million people, "the equivalent of a World War III."[7]

Western history is drenched in militarism, yes. But that is not all of human history. To give just one example:

Three hundred years before Jesus was born, a powerful prince in India, Ashoka, had dominated much of India by military force. After his last big battle, he walked among the dead in the battlefield where a hundred thousand men had fallen and instead of feeling triumph he felt revulsion. He converted to Buddhism and for the next thirty-seven years, he pioneered a new mode of true (not fake) compassionate government. He left a legacy of concern for people, animals, and the environment. He planted orchards and shade trees along roads, encouraged the arts, built rest houses for travelers, water sheds for animals, and he devoted major resources to the poor and the aged and the sick. As futurist Duane Elgin says in his hope-filled book *Promise Ahead: A Vision of Hope and Action for Humanity's Future*, "Ashoka's political administration was marked by the end of war; peace was his policy. His governmental officers were trained as peace-makers "building mutual good will among races, sects, and parties."[8]

The result? His kingdom lasted more than two thousand years until the military empire of Britain invaded India. Britain's empire, based on "superpower thinking," did not last, nor did that of Alexander the Great, Caesar, Genghis Khan, Napoleon, Hitler, or Stalin. Historians have said that among all the monarchs of history, the star of Ashoka shines almost alone. But it need not shine alone. You can almost hear the prophets of Israel crying out to us: "Have you ears and cannot hear? Have you eyes and cannot see?"

Any Hope?

There is hope, lots of it, from two unlikely sources—*embarrassment* and *fear*—and from one likely source, *the emergence of a politics of peacemaking.*

Military power, even "superpower" military power, is being embarrassed, and examples of successful nonviolent modes of resistance are multiplying. Alternatives to military slaughter are being tested and proved. It is slowly dawning on our dull-witted species that *violence is dumb* and rarely produces any good.

With all the bravado of the schoolyard bully flouting his bulging biceps, America has boasted and relied on its "superpower" status, its "nuclear supremacy." That supremacy meant nothing in Vietnam, Iraq, or Afghanistan. September 11, 2001, proved that a handful of men with nothing more than box cutters and penknives as weapons could destroy the Twin Towers and damage the Pentagon, symbols of American economic and military strength. This signaled the end of nation-versus-nation warfare as in World War II. As Karen Armstrong says, "It was an attack against the United States, but it was a warning to all of us in the First World."[9] It made us aware of "a new nakedness and a raw [and new] vulnerability." If our policies inspire hatred around the world, and they do—see *Why Do People Hate America?* by Ziauddin Sardar and Merryl Wyn Davies—the angry of the world have the means to get at us.[10] The National Security Strategy of the United States in 2002 admitted that America is now threatened less by conquering states than by failing ones, "less by fleets and armies than by catastrophic technologies in the hands of the embittered few." A recent estimate by information-warfare specialists at the Pentagon reveals how vulnerable developed nations are. The study estimated that a well-prepared attack by fewer that thirty computer whizzes with a budget of less than ten million dollars "could bring the United States to its knees, shutting down everything from electric power grids to air traffic control centers."[11]

There is no way we can adequately protect our one thousand harbor channels, our 3,700 passenger and cargo terminals, the seven million cargo containers moving in and out of all parts of our ports, factories, and refineries; we cannot protect all our fish farms and megafarms, our chemical plants and nuclear energy facilities. To penetrate any of this is to penetrate us—and they are all penetrable. The idea of protected borders has become obsolete. A single rifle in the hands of two men, John Allen Muhammad and Lee Boyd Malvo, changed life for twenty-two days in the area around our nation's capital in 2002 when they went on a sniping spree. Mere hundreds of trained and motivated persons could paralyze our nation, with catastrophic effect on all commerce.

Atomic devices that fit in a suitcase and can be easily hidden in huge cargo containers are now technically feasible. Angering nations by our aggressive policies motivates those with access to use them and—*your attention please!*—we should expect their use in the United States if present trends continue.

Jesus and the prophets of Israel were realists. Their insight into the weakness of the sword is born out even today. Mohandas Gandhi, Martin Luther King, and Nelson Mandela showed the power of nonviolent resistance. Almost bloodlessly, dictators such as Ferdinand Marcos and at least seven Latin American despots have been driven out. As Walter Wink writes, "In 1989–90 alone fourteen nations underwent nonviolent revolutions. . . ."[12] The freeing of Eastern Europe from Soviet totalitarian control was not achieved by invading armies. Gene Sharp, a historian of resistance movements, lists 198 different types of successful nonviolent actions that are on the historical record, but neglected by historians and journalists who prefer to report on the flash of war.[13] "Britain's Indian colony of three hundred million people was liberated nonviolently at a cost of about eight thousand lives. . . . France's Algerian colony of about ten million was liberated by violence, but it cost almost one million lives."[14] Do the math.

So much for the safety-by-arms myth. Bullying with weapons is counterproductive. The United States has proved that building the biggest arsenal in all of history, invading countries, and placing your military all over the planet makes you more, not less, vulnerable. Nations that don't do that don't fear terrorism. That lesson, if learned by the people and taught to the government, could give grounds for hope.

But What of Humanitarian Military Interventions?

One of deepest convictions that grips our imagination in its steely claws is the belief that the ultimate and surest route to safety is the military. Sure, all kinds of things should be tried, but when the ultimate push comes to the ultimate shove, sound the trumpet, bring on the marines. Did not even Gandhi say that if there were only two choices in the face of evil, cowardice or violence, he would prefer violence?

However, and this is key, there is a third option. It is called peacemaking. It is called nonviolent, intelligent politics, nonviolent strategy. Defenders of "humanitarian military intervention" (with all the oxymoronic implications of that concept) point to cases like Rwanda, where it is argued that military intervention could have prevented genocide. The flaw in this argument is exposed by looking at the years preceding the eruption of violence. A distinguished group of experts put it this way: "Had there been international determination to make the Arusha peace accord work—had there been an amnesty provision in the agreement; a demobilization plan; a genuine attempt to deal with the refugee problem; radio broadcasts to challenge the views of extremists; humanitarian coordination; provision of adequate policing; resources such as riot gear, maps, up-to-date information, early warning systems linked to institutions that could initiate preventative nonviolent action; and a culture of accountability and strong international institutions—the genocide could have been prevented. The failure in Rwanda was a failure of politics—the result of a lack of faith in and commitment to the slow and unglamorous work of nonviolent political action. . . . Military options only seem morally compelling because of a host of lost opportunities."[15]

The problem with "humanitarian military interventionism" is this: arriving late at a long-neglected crisis may create more problems than it solves, adding another set of belligerents to an already over-militarized situation, leaving unattended the complex economic, historical, religious-ethnic, and resource problems that lie at the root of the unrest, and having no realistic plans for follow-up. No matter how you describe such interventions, the fact remains that a so-called humanitarian military intervention is a violent action; and violence, even in the hands of do-gooders, is a lethal weapon. It is a pathetic substitute for the advance work of intelligent diplomacy and peacemaking. In many defenses of military intervention for humanitarian purposes there lurks our illusory confidence in violence as the old reliable standby, always there waiting to solve the problems we have helped to create.

Hypocrisy is always the symptom of iniquity. When warriors claim humanitarian motives, watch out. "Particularly interesting is how 'establishing women's rights' became part of the moral justification given [by President Bush] for waging the 'war on terror.'"[16] The hypocritical claim: "we're doing good things for women, that's what we're about, not oil or empire or selfish things like that."

So Where Is the Hope?

There is hope in disenchantment. There is mounting evidence that war in the twentieth and bloodiest of centuries has made an impression. Soldiering has lost its glamour. The United States dare not institute a draft; it would start a rebellion. Volunteers are being offered bribes to enlist. Americans are learning that their militarily bloated economy and politics are not paying off. The very dollar that symbolized American supremacy is in decline and the United States of America is heavily in debt to (of all nations) the Communist People's Republic of China. China has been conquering global markets while the United States exhausts itself invading other countries. Communist China produces more than 90 percent of Wal-Mart's merchandise.[17] One study predicts that in the near future "there will be a profoundly altered United States: economically weaker and technically less competent, with an impotent currency, rampant corruption, and distant memories of superpower glory."[18] Fear, says the Bible, is the beginning of wisdom. A Russian proverb says that fear has big eyes. Eyes may be opening to alternative modes of power.

Scholars are analyzing alternative modes of power. Not only are people tiring of war but globalization of economies is promoting more interdependence than individual nation-states used to have. That's progress. One study, *Just Peacemaking*, offers, as its subtitle says, "ten practices for abolishing war."[19] Major victories are won by peaceful means, like unilateral initiatives to relieve tension. President Dwight Eisenhower in 1958 announced that the United States would stop above-ground nuclear testing for a year, and longer if the Soviets reciprocated. The Soviets reciprocated and this lasted three years. When testing resumed, President John F. Kennedy initiated it again on his own and "this led to the Atmospheric Test Ban Treaty and the beginning of the thaw of the Cold War."[20] Soviet premiers Yuri Andropov and Mikhail Gorbachev offered further unilateral initiatives that contributed to the wind-down of tensions. These moves are not wildly idealistic; they work.

There was pressure in India for war to end the British occupation. Gandhi pushed ahead with nonviolent moves and he won: the British left.

It has often been suggested—but not acted on—that we have a cabinet-level Department of Peace to work full time on initiatives to spot and work on tensions that could lead to war. Instead, we have a Department of War, euphemistically named "Defense." (It once was called, more honestly, the War Department.)

Hope from New Fears

A term from science is making its way to the front page: *positive feedback loop*. It relates to the big melt that is now ongoing due to global climate change. The concept is as simple as it is terrifying. As global warming increases, ice melts at the poles. Bare ground absorbs three times as much heat as ice and this melts more ice, and so it goes. Optimists feel we could with an effort comparable to a world war stymie this process. Pessimists feel the "tipping point" has been passed and oceans may eventually rise as much as twenty-three feet, rewriting the geography of the planet. The Ministry of Tourism on the Maldive Islands in the Indian Ocean is advertising, "Come and see us while we're still here." At the Rio Earth Summit in 1992, Maldive President Maumoon Abdul Gayoom stated that "a few feet of rise is the end of our country." The waters of the sea are slowly claiming the Maldives. There is wide and widening agreement that human activity is a major factor in generating this heat.

Physics professor Marty Hoffert worries that if "we're not going to solve global warming, the earth is going to become an ecological disaster, and somebody will visit in a few hundred million years and find there were some intelligent beings who lived here for a while, but they just couldn't handle the transition from being hunter-gatherers to high technology."[21]

Hope is rising from the powerful emotion of *fear*. We are at a crucial moment of fear shifting. We have been distracted by the wrong enemies. The enemy is not "terrorism," "communism," or the barbarian hordes that worried our forebears; the enemy is *us*, as the medical condition of our planet moves from "serious" to "critical." It is not arms but brains that are our last best defense. Armies won't solve but will instead contribute to the massive global problem we face and people are finally noticing. Polls now show that well over 80 percent of people admit the global warming problem is real and that there is a need to take immediate action. Diverting military spending from imagined threats to this real threat is our prime need. Since global warming threatens everyone, there is new reason for an international ecumenism. Shared fear can make friends of former foes.

The problem is that we fall in love with our enmities. The poet C. P. Cavafy spoke of that when he wrote: "Night is here but the barbarians have not come. Some people arrived from the frontiers, and they said that there are no

longer any barbarians. . . ." Somewhat wist-
fully he adds, "These people were a kind of
solution."[22] It's easier to worry about what we
know than to face emerging terrors. Also, we
can deny the truly horrible just as we shy away
from looking directly at the sun. And yet the
truly horrible is bursting through in our hurricanes, typhoons, and proliferating droughts.
This kind of realistic fear of planetary destruction can be antidotal to our military addic-
tions.

4

Our Love Affair with Violence: "Is You Is or Is You Ain't My Baby?"

The scientist Jacob Bronowski faced a question on the ultimate fate of humanity one night in 1945 when he was driven in a Jeep through the ashy ruins of Nagasaki. In the dark, he had not sensed that they had moved from the open country to the "city." The "city" was a dark and desolate ruin. The only sound he heard was that of an American military radio playing the popular tune "Is You Is or Is You Ain't Ma Baby?" In the context the question was a piercing one. What Bronowski saw in this peak moment of truth was "civilization face to face with its own implications. The implications are both the industrial slum that Nagasaki was before it was bombed, and the ashy desolation that the bomb made of the slum. And civilization asks of both ruins, 'Is You Is or Is You Ain't Ma Baby?'"[1]

The Bible asks the same question and it is equivocal in its answer. On the dismal side: "The

LORD looks down from heaven on all humankind
to see if any act wisely. . . . But all are disloyal,
all are rotten to the core; not one does anything
good, no, not even one" (Ps. 14:2-3). Not a good
prognosis. But then, in a triumph of hope over
experience, Isaiah puts these extravagant prom-
ises into the mouth of God:

> For behold, I create new heavens and a new
> earth. Former things shall no more be remem-
> bered nor shall they be called to mind. . . .
> Weeping and cries for help shall never again
> be heard. . . . Men shall build houses and live
> to inhabit them, plant vineyards and eat their
> fruit. . . . They shall not toil in vain or raise
> children for misfortune. . . . The wolf and the
> lamb shall feed together and the lion shall eat
> straw like cattle. They shall not hurt of destroy
> in all my holy mountain, says the Lord.
> (Isa. 65:17-25)

For this to happen, violence must yield to
justice. Nothing less than the end of militarism
is anticipated: "All the boots of trampling soldiers and the garments fouled with blood shall
become a burning mass, fuel for fire" (Isa.
9:5). The song of the military will be silenced
(Isa. 25:5). The resulting peace will last "from
now and for evermore" (Isa. 9:7). All of nature
will benefit. Parched deserts will "flower with
fields of asphodel and rejoice and shout for
joy" (Isa. 35:2). This vision of peace is to be
"a light to the nations [shining all the way] to
earth's farthest bounds" (Isa. 49:6).

The Lost Talent of Weeping

The tearless are the enemies of peace because they do not respond appropriately to the evils that peacemaking must address. Tears, after all, are very Christic. In that beautiful text from Luke, Jesus looked at the city, and he wept, heartbroken over the fact that we do not know the things that make for peace (Luke 19:41:42). Jeremiah said that unless your eyes run with tears you will come to a terrible ruin (Jer. 9:18-19). I was amazed, as a young Catholic boy, when I saw on the back of the *Missale Romanum* a prayer for the gift of tears. And it said, "Oh God, strike into the *duritiam*, the hardness of my heart, and bring forth a saving flood of tears." And as a little boy, I thought, "Who wants tears, when you grow up you don't have them anymore, especially if you are a man?" And that precisely is the problem. If you are without tears, it is a tragedy. You are not Christic. You are not human. "How blest are you who weep . . ." (Luke 6:21). Jesus wept. He looked at that city and said, "If only you knew the things that make for your peace, but you don't." And he broke down sobbing.

Let us update that text. Let us hear Jesus say, "America, America, if only you knew the things that make for your peace, if only you could see that the answer is not in your weaponry and economic muscle. If only I could, like a mother hen, wrap my wings around you, wings of justice and peace and compassion, if you could use your great talent and wealth to work to end world hunger, world thirst, world illiteracy, no one would hate you, no one would crash planes into your buildings, you would know shalom. That's the promise of Isaiah 32:17. Plant justice and compassion, and then, and only then, will peace grow. Then you could burn those chariots in a holy fire and you would be secure."

There is an illness in this land of ours that makes the Bible's peacemaking message "a hard saying." I'll call it ICS: Imperial Comfort Syndrome. When you are living in an extremely advantaged imperial situation, basking in unearned and purloined privileges as we are in the United States, you become very comfortable. This particular illness, ICS, does not result in fever or in cold chills. Its symptoms are tepidity and a dull, crippling kind of depression. It causes such things as this: in many recent elections as many as 60 percent of eligible American voters didn't even show up at the polls. That is the sickness of ICS: Imperial Comfort Syndrome. For an searing indictment of it, I would take you to Revelation 3:15, 22, and let us rend our hearts and listen. The author puts these words into the mouth of God: "I know all your ways. You are neither hot nor cold. How I wish you were either hot or cold. But because you are lukewarm, neither hot nor cold, I will spit you out of my mouth. . . . Hear, you who have ears to hear, what the Spirit says to the churches."

We may be a doomed species, destined for a short tenure in this little corner of the universe. Or, having exhausted violence and war, we could embrace our possibilities for peace. We, as a species, have moved out of some of our earlier barbarities. As anthropologist Ralph Linton observes, moral concern in our early years was limited to kith and kin. Members of other tribes were even seen as a legitimate source of meat.[2] In ancient Greece, even murder did not always conflict with social respectability. "Outside the circle of the dead man's kinsmen and friends, there is no indication of any popular sentiment against ordinary homicide."[3] After centuries of assuming that slavery was a normal necessity of life, we grew to see it as an aberration.

It is in us to outgrow war. The formula is easy enough: put your main trust in justice, not weapons, trust life-power more than kill-power, specialize in diplomacy and imagination, not bludgeoning. That hoped for flowering of conscience may seem but a dream but, to adapt the words of the Irish poet William Butler Yeats, tread softly if you would tread on that dream!

Notes

Preface

1. J. Glenn Gray, *The Warriors: Reflections on Men in Battle* (New York: Harper & Row, 1959), 204.

Chapter One

1. Chris Hedges, *What Every Person Should Know about War* (New York: Free Press, 2003), 1.

2. L. F. Richardson, *Statistics of Deadly Quarrels* (Pacific Grove, CA: Boxwood Press, 1960). Quoted in Vaclav Smil, "The Next 50 Years: Fatal Discontinuities," *Population and Development Review* 31, no. 2 (June, 2005): 225. B. Hayes, "Statistics of Deadly Quarrels," *American Scientist* 90 (2002): 15.

3. Charter of the United Nations and Statute of the International Court of Justice, published by The United Nations, Department of Public Information, Reprint DPI/511, October 1997.

4. Richard Falk, "Why International Law Matters," *The Nation* 276, no. 9 (March 10, 2003): 20.

5. These ideas are developed in Glen H. Stassen, ed., *Just Peacemaking: Ten Practices for Abolishing War* (Cleveland: Pilgrim Press, 1998), 146–55. This is not just a "pipe dream": peace actions work. In one year, 1994, for example, there were seventeen peacekeeping operations to which seventy-six nations contributed.

6. Gene Sharp, *The Politics of Nonviolent Action: Part One: Power and Struggle* (Boston: Porter Sargent, 1973), 73.

7. Barbara Ehrenreich, *Blood Rites: Origins and History of the Passions of War* (New York: Henry Holt, 1997), 177–78.

8. Ibid.

9. Quoted in Lawrence H. Keeley, *War before Civilization: The Myth of the Peaceful Savage* (New York: Oxford University Press, 1996), 74.

10. Michael Walzer, *Just and Unjust Wars: A Moral Argument with Historical Illustrations* (New York: Basic Books, 1977), 36.

11. Gray, *The Warriors,* 138.

12. S. I. A. Marshall, *Men against Fire* (Norman: University of Oklahoma Press, 2000), chaps. 5 and 6.

13. Howard Zinn, *A People's History of the United States: 1492 to the Present,* revised and updated edition (New York: Harper Perennial, 1995), 80.

14. Ehrenreich, *Blood Rites,* 188.

15. Walzer, *Just and Unjust Wars,* 138–43.

16. Quoted in ibid., 140.

17. Robert Jewett and John Shelton Lawrence, *Captain America and the Crusade against Evil: The Dilemma of Zealous Nationalism* (Grand Rapids, MI: Wm. B. Eerdmans, 2003), 43.

18. Andrew J. Bacevich, *The New American Militarism: How Americans Are Seduced by War* (New York: Oxford University Press, 2005), 1.

19. Quoted in Zinn, *A People's History,* 158.

20. Walter Sullivan, *We Are Not Alone* (New York: Signet, 1966), 245.

21. Erich Fromm, *The Anatomy of Human Destructiveness* (New York: Holt, Rinehart, and Winston, 1973), 105.

22. Clyde Prestowitz, *Rogue Nation: American Unilateralism and the Failure of Good Intentions* (New York: Basic Books, 2003), 26.

23. Andrew J. Bacevich, *The New American Militarism: How Americans Are Seduced by War* (New York Oxford University Press), 215. See *Worldwide Military Expenditures* at http://www.globalsecurity.org/military/world/spending.htm (December 2006). A demilitarized foreign policy that did not require keeping forces in 150 countries around the world would free up several hundred billion dollars for social and peacemaking purposes. See Howard Zinn on estimates by Randall Forsberg, an expert on military expenditures. *A People's History,* 632–33.

24. See Adolph Reed, Jr., "A GI Bill for Everybody," *Dissent* 48, no. 4 (Fall 2001).

25. Bacevich, *The New American Militarism,* 32.

26. Desmond Tutu, "Stop Killing the Children," *The Washington Post,* November 24, 1996, C7.

Chapter Two

1. Augustine, *Epis.* 138, ii, 15.

2. There is an axiom in ethics: *bonum ex integra causa: malum ex quocumque defectu.* That means: failure on any of the essentials makes the action (or project) unjust, even though on many other counts it may look morally promising. Each of the tests of the "just-war theory" is an essential.

3. *The Challenge of Peace: God's Promise and Our Response, A Pastoral Letter on War and Peace,* May 3, 1983, National Conference of Catholic Bishops, Publication No. 863, U.S. Catholic Conference.

4. Walzer, *Just and Unjust Wars,* 299.

5. See the call to the Christian churches to fulfill a political and prophetic role in national decisions and conduct of war in Daniel M. Bell, Jr., "Can a War Against Terrorism Be Just?: Or, What is Just War Good For?" *Cross Currents* 56, no. 1 (Spring 2006): 34–45.

6. David Hollenbach, *Nuclear Ethics: A Christian Moral Argument* (New York: Paulist Press, 1983), 39.

7. Quoted in David Armstrong, "Dick Cheney's Song of America: Drafting a Plan for Global Dominance," *Harper's* 305, no. 1824 (October 1, 2002): 76–82.

8. Commencement speech by George W. Bush at West Point Academy, June 1, 2002. See http://www.whitehouse.gov/news/releases/2002/06/20020601-3.html (December 2006).

9. The National Security Strategy of the United States of America, September 2002. See http://www.whitehouse.gov/nsc/nss.html (December 2006).

10. See Clyde Prestowitz, *Rogue Nation: American Unilateralism and the Failure of Good Intentions* (New York: Basic Books, 2003), 22–24.

11. Ibid., 23. The Westphalian model assumed separate states; and this is no longer the case given the interlocking of capital, manufacturing, and shifting alliances. See Michael Joseph Smith, "Strengthen the United Nations and International Efforts for Cooperation and Human Rights," in *Just Peacemaking: Ten Practices for Abolishing War*, ed. Glen H. Stassen (Cleveland: Pilgrim Press, 1998), 146–55.

12. See Daniel C. Maguire, "The Empire/Servility Syndrome," *A Moral Creed for All Christians* (Minneapolis: Fortress Press, 2005), chap. one. See also William Blum, *Rogue State: A Guide to the World's Only Superpower* (Monroe, MD: Common Courage Press, 2000); and Chalmers Johnson, *Blowback: The Costs and Consequences of American Empire* (New York: Holt, 2000). Johnson's book, written two years before September 11, 2001, predicted "blowback" (a CIA term) from Osama bin Laden due to U.S. presence and policies vis-à-vis the Middle East. There

are various ways to "overthrow" a government, by subversion or by war. Hence, the figures vary. Stephen Kinzer puts the number of governments overthrown at fourteen: "The invasion of Iraq in 2003 was not an isolated episode. It was the culmination of a 110-year period during which Americans overthrew fourteen governments that displeased them for various ideological, political, and economic reasons." See *Overthrow: America's Century of Regime Change from Hawaii to Iraq* (New York: Henry Holt, 2006), 1.

13. If a government has lost all legitimacy, a revolution may be instigated, when all nonviolent means of resistance have been exhausted and when sufficient legitimacy attaches to an emerging authority. The successes of nonviolent revolutions are discussed below.

14. See Robert Previdi, "America's Path to War," *The Long-Term View* (Massachusetts School of Law at Andover) 6, no. 2: 104.

15. Michael Walzer, *Just and Unjust Wars,* 118. This war is not a good example of the policing paradigm since the United States went beyond policing and turned vigilante when it crossed the 38th parallel. Also, the action was unilateral, not collective, as envisioned in the U.N. Charter. Ibid., 117–124.

16. Howard Zinn, *A People's History of the United States: 1492 to the Present,* revised and updated edition (New York: Harper Perennial, 1995), 467.

17. In 1973, sensing the mess it was making, Congress passed the War Powers Resolution, which was also a violation of the Constitution since it allowed the President to free-wheel it for sixty days without congressional involvement. This also has been ignored as the monarchical presidency assumes sovereign power.

18. Anne Frank, *The Diary of a Young Girl,* trans. B. M. Mooyaart (Garden City, NY: Doubleday, 1953), 201.

19. Bruce Russett, "Advance Democracy, Human Rights, and Religious Liberty," in Stassen, ed., *Just Peacemaking,* 97, 106.

20. Human and animal sacrifice is a persistent part of history. The idea was that sacrificing animals, and better yet, humans to the gods, brought security to the rest of us. It is hard to believe that this is not still operative at some level as people cheer and honor our "fallen dead." When Mesha, the king of the Moabites, saw his troops losing, he took his eldest son "and offered him as a whole-offering upon the city wall" (2 Kings 3:27). Are we still offering our sons and daughters on the wall of senseless wars in the spirit of Mesha? René Girard argues that wars are "merely another form of sacrificial violence." René Girard, *Violence and the Sacred* (Baltimore: Johns Hopkins University Press, 1979), 251.

21. Ibid., 249.

22. Nicholas Berdyaev, *The Destiny of Man* (New York: Harper & Row, 1960), 60.

23. Roland de Vaux, *Ancient Israel,* vol. I (New York: McGraw-Hill, 1965), 11. Girard, in his *Violence and the Sacred,* shows that sometimes the malefactor was spared and some innocent person was killed to make satisfaction in order to break the cycle of vengeance. This may seem primitive in the pejorative sense, but its purpose was peace. They wanted to show that it was not just quid pro quo vengeance. Their fear was of the Hatfield/McCoy self-destructive vortex of vengeance.

24. Ernest Becker, *Angel in Armor: A Post-Freudian Perspective on the Nature of Man* (New York: Braziller, 1969), 111–14.

25. Karl Popper, *The Open Society and Its Enemies* (Princeton, NJ: Princeton University Press, 1950), 119–20.

26. Arnold Toynbee, *Change and Habit: The Challenge of Our Time* (New York: Oxford University Press, 1966), 112.

27. Norman K. Gottwald, *The Tribes of Yahweh: A Sociology of the Religion of Liberated Israel, 1250–1050 B.C.E.* (Maryknoll, NY: Orbis Books, 1979), 640.

28. Quoted by Winslow T. Wheeler, "The Week of Shame: Congress Wilts as the President Demands an Unclogged Road to War" (Washington, DC: Center for Defense Information, January, 2003), 17. See Chalmers Johnson, *The Sorrows of Empire: Militarism, Secrecy, and the End of the Republic* (New York: Henry Holt, 2004).

29. Barbara Ehrenreich, *Blood Rites: Origins and History of the Passions of War* (New York: Henry Holt, 1997), 11.

30. *The Challenge of Peace*, 30. See also Michael Walzer, *Just and Unjust Wars*, 266–67.

31. Roland H. Bainton, *Christian Attitudes toward War and Peace: A Historical Survey and Critical Re-evaluation* (New York and Nashville: Abingdon Press, 1960), 216–19.

32. Ibid., 218–19. Emphasis mine.

33. Zinn, *A People's History*, 75–76.

34. Ibid, 249. This class bias continues today. A report in *Foreign Policy* (September/October 2004), 17, says: "The Pentagon does not keep information on the socioeconomic status of recruits, but evidence suggests that the lower middle class (regardless of race) bears a disproportionate burden." The most disadvantaged are kept out of the military due to the requirement of a high school education, but "the biggest predictor of whether you're in the military

today is the unemployment rate in your home country." See also, Bob Deans, in *Atlanta Journal-Constitution*, November 2, 2006, 12A: "A study released in September by the National Priorities Project found that young men and women from families with household incomes ranging between $30,000 and $60,000 a year are over-represented in Army recruitment levels. As income levels rise above $60,000 a year, representation drops off steadily, the study showed."

35. Quoted in ibid., 58.

36. David M. Kennedy, "The Best Army We Can Buy," *New York Times,* July 25, 2005, A23.

37. Chris Hedges, *What Every Person Should Know about War* (New York: Free Press, 2003), 7.

38. Laurie Ann Mazur and Susan E. Sechler, "Global Interdependence and the Need for Social Stewardship," Paper No. 1, Global Interdependence Initiative, Rockefeller Brother Fund, 1997, 10–11.

39. Zinn, *A People's History,* 414.

40. Robert J. Art and Kenneth N. Waltz, eds., *The Use of Force: International Politics and Foreign Policy* (Boston: Little, Brown, 1971), 331. The Soviets had already engulfed Rumania, Bulgaria, Yugoslavia, Czechoslovakia, and Hungary and the argument was made to use the atomic bomb "to make Russia more manageable in Europe."

41. Walzer, *Just and Unjust Wars,* 198.

42. Quoted in ibid., 261.

43. Ibid., 255.

44. Quoted in Zinn, *A People's History,* 413.

45. S. V. Viswanatha, "International Law in Ancient India," quote in Walzer, *Just and Unjust Wars,* 43.

46. Walzer, *Just and Unjust Wars,* 160.

47. Ibid., 168.

48. Daniel C. Maguire, *The New Subversives: Anti-Americanism of the Religious Right* (New York: Continuum, 1982), 93.

49. Quoted in Bainton, *Christian Attitudes toward War and Peace*, 110.

50. Stanley Windass, *Christianity versus Violence: A Social and Historical Study of War and Christianity* (London: Sheed and Ward, 1964), 43.

51. "Pastoral Constitution on the Church in the Modern World," No. 80., in Walter M. Abbot, S.J. gen. ed., *The Documents of Vatican II* (New York: Herder & Herder, 1966), 293–94.

52. Ehrenreich, "The Ecstasy of War," *Blood Rites*, 7–22.

53. R. W. Apple, "War: Bush's Presidential Rite of Passage," *New York Times*, December 21, 1989, A1.

54. David Hume, *Enquiry Concerning the Principles of Morals*, Section III, Part I.

55. Francesco de Vitoria, *De Indis et De Iure Belli Relationes*, quoted in Michael Walzer, *Just and Unjust Wars,* 39. Vitoria was not a fringe figure in the history of the law of war. He became a major influence on the slowly developing international law of war, and his influence is cited even in the Universal Declaration of Human Rights of the United Nations.

56. Quoted in Walzer, *Just and Unjust Wars,* 134.

57. For a fuller explanation of the Principle of Double Effect, see Daniel C. Maguire, *The Moral Choice* (Garden City, NY: Doubleday, 1978), 163–67.

58. Henry Davis, S.J., *Moral and Pastoral Theology*, Vol. 2, sixth ed. (London and New York: Sheed and Ward, 1949), 150.

59. Ibid.

60. Ibid.

61. Quoted in Bainton, *Christian Attitudes toward War and Peace*, 234.

62. *The Challenge of Peace*, 31.

63. William V. O'Brien, *The Conduct of Just and Limited War* (New York: Praeger, 1981), 27.

64. Henk W. Houweling, "The Epidemiology of War, 1816–1980," *Journal of Conflict Resolution* 29, no. 4 (1985): 641–63.

65. René Girard, *Violence and the Sacred* (Baltimore: The Johns Hopkins University Press, 1979), 26.

66. Ehrenreich, *Blood Rites,* 143.

67. Maguire, *A Moral Creed for All Christians*, 79–80. See Graca Machel, *The Impact of War on Children* (London: Hurst & Company, 2001).

68. Jim Wallis, *God's Politics: Why the Right Gets It Wrong and the Left Doesn't Get It* (San Francisco: HarperSanFrancisco, 2005), 263–63.

69. Joseph J. Fahey, *War and the Christian Conscience* (Maryknoll, NY: Orbis Books, 2005), 110.

70. Quoted in Michael Walzer, *Just and Unjust Wars*, 162.

71. Associated Press report, May 29, 2006.

Chapter Three

1. See Jack Nelson-Pallmeyer, *Is Religion Killing Us? Violence in the Bible and the Qur'an* (New York: Continuum, 2003); Matthias Beier, *A Violent God-Image: An Introduction to the Work of Eugen Drewermann* (New York: Continuum, 2004); Regina M. Schwartz, *The Curse of Cain: The Violent Legacy of Monotheism* (Chicago: University of Chicago Press, 1997).

2. Abraham Heschel, *The Prophets* (Philadelphia: Jewish Publication Society of America, 1962), 166.

3. Walter Brueggemann, *Revelation and Violence* (Milwaukee: Marquette University Press, 1986), 25–26.

4. Walter Wink, *Engaging the Powers: Disarmament and Resistance in a World of Domination* (Minneapolis: Fortress Press, 1992), 175–93.

5. Mahatma Gandhi, in *Harijan*, March 10, 1946, quoted in Mark Juergensmeyer, *Fighting with Gandhi: A Step-by-Step Strategy for Resolving Everyday Conflicts* (San Francisco: HarperCollins, 1986), 43.

6. Robert Nisbet, *The Social Philosophers: Community and Conflict in Western Thought* (New York: Thomas Y. Crowell, 1973), 11.

7. "The World at War—January 2002," *The Defense Monitor* 31, no. 1 (January 2002).

8. Duane Elgin, *Promise Ahead: A Vision of Hope and Action for Humanity's Future* (New York: HarperCollins, 2000), 117.

9. Karen Armstrong, *The Battle for God* (New York: Ballantine Books, 2001), vi.

10. Ziauddin Srdar and Merryl Wyn Davies, *Why Do People Hate America?* (New York: The Disinformation Company, 2002). See http://www.disinfo.com (December 2006). The press calls itself "disinformation" to mock the false consolations offered to us by our government and by the mainstream journalistic media.

11. Elgin, *Promise Ahead,* 110.

12. Walter Wink, *Jesus and Nonviolence: A Third Way* (Minneapolis: Fortress Press, 2003), 1–2.

13. Gene Sharp, *The Politics of Nonviolent Action*, 3 vols. (Boston: Porter Sargent, 1973–1975).

14. Ibid., 52. On nonviolence teaching in world religions, see Daniel L. Smith-Christopher, ed., *Subverting Hatred: The Challenge of Nonviolence in Religious Traditions* (Maryknoll, NY: Orbis, 2000).

15. Stanley Hauerwas, Linda Hogan, and Enda McDonagh, "The Case for Abolition of War in the Twenty-First Century," *Journal of the Society of Christian Ethics* 25, no. 2 (Fall/Winter 2005): 31. The Gulf War of 1991 is touted as an exemplary U.S. military triumph. But as Alan Geyer notes, the war was brought on not only by Saddam's blundering aggression but also by the "United States' lack of meaningful political memory of its past policies and actions that contributed to the hostilities." See Geyer, "Acknowledge Responsibility for Conflict and Injustice and Seek Repentance and Forgiveness," in *Just Peacemaking: Ten Practices for Abolishing War*, ed. Glen H. Stassen (Cleveland: Pilgrim Press, 1998), 83.

16. Ibid., 34 n.32. The European Union, intent on economic development, stood by in the 1990s "to watch the slaughter of tens of thousands and the displacement of millions in the Balkan wars." U.S. interventions "on behalf of Muslim Bosnians and Kosovars prevented more death." Vaclav Smil, "The Next 50 Years: Unfolding Trends," *Population and Development Review* 31, no. 4: 609. Once again, a military action responding to neglect.

17. Smil, "The Next 50 Years," 621.

18. Ibid., 632.

19 Stassen, ed., *Just Peacemaking.*

20. Ibid., 48.

21. Quoted in Elizabeth Kolbert, "Annals of Science: The Climate of Man," *The New Yorker*, May 9, 2005, 57.

22. C. P. Cavofy, quoted in Edmund Stillman and William Pfaff, The Politics of Hysteria (New York: Harper & Row, 1964), 5.

Chapter Four

1. Jacob Bronowski, *Science and Human Values* (New York: Harper & Row, 1965), 3–4.

2. Ralph Linton, "The Problem of Universal Values," in Robert F. Spencer, ed., *Method and Perspective in Anthropology: Papers in Honor of Wilson D. Wallis* (Minneapolis: University of Minnesota Press, 1954), 157.

3. Robert J. Bonner, and Gertrude Smith, *The Administration of Justice from Homer to Aristotle* (Chicago: University of Chicago Press, 1930), 16.